The Easy
Edible
Mushroom
Guide

.......y retired as
Head of Mycology at the Royal Botanic
Gardens, Kew, after almost 40 years of
continuous study of the world's mushrooms.
Among his popular books on fungi are *The
Mitchell Beazley Pocket Guide to Mushrooms*
and the *Larousse Fieldguide to Mushrooms*.

The Easy
Edible
Mushroom
Guide

Written by
David Pegler

Britain and Europe

Paintings by John Wilkinson
and Gill Tomblin

AURUM PRESS

First published in Great Britain by Aurum Press Ltd
25, Bedford Avenue, London WC1B 3AT

A catalogue record for this book as available from the British Library

ISBN 1 85410 631 7

| Originated by | Chroma Graphics (Overseas) Pte. Ltd. |
| Printed in Italy by | Grafedit |

Conceived, edited, designed and produced by
Duncan Petersen Publishing, 31, Ceylon Road, London W14 OPY

Editorial Director	Andrew Duncan
Art Director	Mel Petersen
Text by	David Pegler
Paintings by	John Wilkinson; poisonous species by Gill Tomblin
Photographs by	Gordon Dickson, Alan R. Outen, A.W. Brand, Harry Smith Collection, A-Z Botanical, NHPA, Professor Giovanni Pacioni, Jens H. Petersen
Recipes by	Fiona Duncan and Lucinda Cookson
Editorial Assistants	Nicola Davies, Sarah Barlow
Design Assistant	Beverly Stewart

Contents

An introduction to fungi

Yellow swamp brittle gill

Everybody has an opinion about wild mushrooms. To some, they are either poisonous or to be feared because of their association with decay and death. The overnight appearance of mushrooms has long been linked with magic and the devil. Others will trample mushrooms, believing a 'pest' will be eliminated, little understanding their biology and manner of growth. Yet there is no reason to fear mushrooms any more than plants: for certain plants can also be deadly if eaten, whilst others are delicious. Mushrooms, like fruits, cannot be picked randomly, and it is essential to be able to recognize a few favourite species.

In Britain, and in many Anglo-Saxon based countries, there has, for centuries, been an innate fear of mushrooms, known as mycophobia. On the other hand, most of Continental Europe comprises mycophilic countries, in which mushroom hunting is a universal pastime and a major autumn activity. An English doctor, Charles Badham, gained a fascination for edible fungi whilst living in Rome. On his return in 1847, he published *The Esculent Funguses of England*', a work which introduced to the British palate many edible species that had long been enjoyed in Italy. In his opening remarks, he commented that 'no country is perhaps richer in esculent funguses than our own ... no market might therefore be better supplied than the English, and yet England is the only country in Europe where this important and savoury food is, from ignorance or prejudice, left to perish ungathered'. This contrasted with many European countries where large numbers of trained 'consultants', accredited mushroom pickers, were employed, and with the extensive selling of wild mushrooms in markets.

Mankind has shown a fascination for the kingdom Fungi throughout history, and some of our oldest artefacts and writings illustrate fungi. Hieroglyphics painted during the time of Akkuut (BC2700) illustrated edible mushrooms. Chinese mushroom cultivation probably dates back even further. In Ancient Greece, the dramatist Eurypides (BC484-406) considered poisonous fungi, whilst Theophrastus (BC370-287), described truffles. At the time of the Holy Roman Empire, a fungus called 'Agaricum', which is the bracket fungus, *Laricifomes officinale*, was mentioned and described by both Dioscorides (50-70AD, *De Materia Medica*) and Pliny the Elder (23-79AD, *Naturalis Historia*), and was widely used and imported from Russia for its 'medicinal' properties. It contains agaricic acid, which acts as a purgative, thus providing a 'universal remedy'. It was still extensively commented upon by the herbalists Mattioli (1560) and Cesalpino (1583) during the Italian Renaissance. Pliny the Elder described at least six edible mushrooms in sufficient detail for them to be easily identified today.

Nowadays, mushroom hunting can become very much a family activity, and can soon result in favourite collecting areas becoming a closely guarded secret. Mushroom hunting and identification is a satisfying and rewarding activity in itself, but mushrooms may be used in many different ways. They are used in floral arrangements, for making natural dyes, and they are interesting subjects for painting and photography. They have a long history of medicinal use. They figure in religious cults, and they are often misused for so-called recreational purposes. Most of all, mushrooms are collected for the pot.

Remember, however, never to take a risk with a wild mushroom. Before going further with this guide, study and understand the safety code on page 252.

Mushroom biology

What is a fungus?

Animals and plants are 'cellular' in their structure, that is to say they are formed by cells, but mushrooms and other fungi are composed of thin filaments. These filaments, called hyphae (hypha, singular), are tubular and microscopical, generally about 3-10 thousands (µm) of one millimetre wide, with the walls made of chitin, the same organic substance that forms the protective body coverings of insects. The hyphae lengthen and frequently branch to a weft which is known as

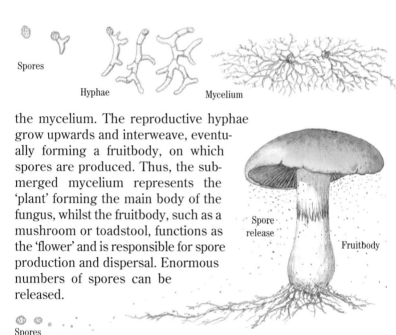

Spores

Hyphae

Mycelium

the mycelium. The reproductive hyphae grow upwards and interweave, eventually forming a fruitbody, on which spores are produced. Thus, the submerged mycelium represents the 'plant' forming the main body of the fungus, whilst the fruitbody, such as a mushroom or toadstool, functions as the 'flower' and is responsible for spore production and dispersal. Enormous numbers of spores can be released.

Spore release

Fruitbody

Spores

Fungi also differ from plants, which manufacture their food, and animals which ingest and internally digest their food, in that they secrete enzymes and digest their food externally. They represent a separate and very large kingdom of their own.

What is a mushroom?

A mushroom (or agaric) is an umbrella-shaped fungus fruitbody, characteristic of the order *Agaricales* in the subdivision *Basidiomycota*. The distinction between a mushroom and a toadstool has no scientific basis. Most mushrooms grow directly from the soil; others may be found on plant debris, on living or dead wood, or are parasitic on other mushrooms. They arise from an underground mycelium and, providing sufficient nutrients and water are present, a new crop will form at each season. The mycelium may continue to grow for hundreds of years or only for a few months. 'Mushrooms' function to produce and disseminate reproductive spores.

Mushroom

Mycelium

How do mushrooms grow?

Mushroom growth – the appearance of fruitbodies overnight – has led to superstition and folklore tales about their supposed magical properties. The reality is less sensational. Animals and plants grow by a slow and complex process of cells dividing and multiplying. In the case of the fungus, most of the hyphal-units are produced within the early stages of the fruitbody formation, and this is scarcely observ-

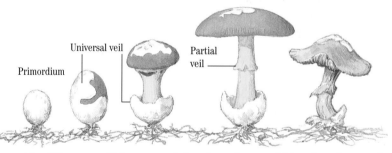

Primordium

Universal veil

Partial veil

able. When conditions are right, there is a rapid intake of water by these hyphae which expand, enabling the fully mature fruitbody to swell up and appear within a few hours. The high water content of the fruitbody also means that it is likely to wilt and decay within a short time. Fruitbody production therefore requires a supply of water, and this is the main factor which determines their occurrence and frequency.

Mushroom biology

Mushroom form and structure

A mushroom undergoes substantial changes during its short life, losing early developmental structures and acquiring new structures. In addition, a mushroom, unlike a plant, lacks any structural tissues and therefore the appearance is subject to the weather and other environmental factors. In order to identify a mushroom correctly, it is essential that the picker must first understand its structure and the manner in which it develops. The button-stage (*primordium*) develops into three main structures, namely the cap (*pileus*), the stem (*stipe*), and the gills (*lamellae*). In certain forms there may be one or more protective veils.

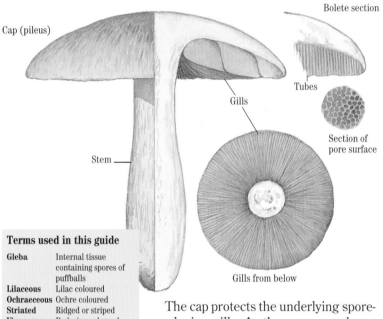

Cap (pileus)

Bolete section

Tubes

Gills

Section of pore surface

Stem

Gills from below

Terms used in this guide

Gleba	Internal tissue containing spores of puffballs
Lilaceous	Lilac coloured
Ochraeceous	Ochre coloured
Striated	Ridged or striped
Vinaceous	Red wine coloured
Violaceous	Violet coloured
Volva	Remains of universal veil at stem base

See also other definitions given in these two pages

The cap protects the underlying spore-producing gills. As the cap expands, so the edge separates from the stem and curves upwards, exposing the gills. The cap surface may develop specialized structures and pigments. The stem raises the cap and gills above the substratum so that the spores can be dispersed. Although the stem is the first structure to be formed, it does not lengthen until after the cap and gills are fully mature. The gills are thin, vertical, radiating plates on the underside of the cap. Often, smaller gills are formed in between the primary gills. The surface of the gills is covered by the spore-producing layer (the *hymenium*).

A helpful aid to identification in the field is the way in which the gills are joined to the top of the stem. There are particular terms to explain these: *adnate* means that the gills are attached by the full gill width; *adnexed* means that the gills only reach the very top

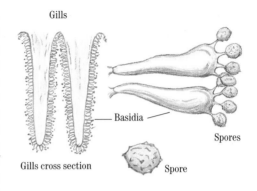

Gills

Basidia

Spores

Gills cross section

Spore

of the stem; *free* indicates that the gills do not reach the stem; *sinuate* gills curve upwards before reaching the stem, then downwards; *decurrent* means that the gill attachment runs down the stem.

Adnate   Adnexed   Free   Sinuate   Decurrent

Protective veil layers are present in some mushrooms. The full complement of layers may be found on some species of the genus *Amanita*. The universal veil envelops the immature fruitbody but on expansion it breaks down, forming the cap scales and a cup-like volva at the stem base. The partial veil covers the immature gills before breaking down to form a ring on the stem. The *hymenium* covers the surfaces of the gills, comprising a single layer of club-shaped cells, the *basidia*, which typically form four *basidiospores*.

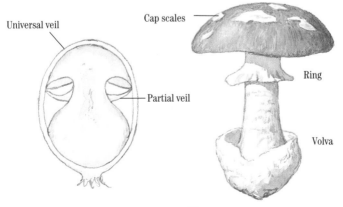

Universal veil

Cap scales

Partial veil

Ring

Volva

A mushroom calendar

The following seasonal lists indicate the appearance of the principal edible and poisonous mushrooms during the year. Some mushrooms have a much longer growing season than others and therefore might be found at any time.

Spring

Spring months will vary within Europe, coming later in northerly and mountainous areas. The Spring crop is dominated by the morels and the St. Georges's mushroom.

Chicken of the woods *(page 140)* MAY-SEPTEMBER
Common morel *(page 148)* APRIL-MAY
Glistening ink cap *(page 108)* APRIL-OCTOBER
Orange peel *(page 154)* MAY-OCTOBER
Shaggy ink cap *(page 106)* APRIL-NOVEMBER
Southern poplar mushroom *(page 48)* MAY-NOVEMBER
St George's mushroom *(page 74)* APRIL-JUNE
Two-toned scale head *(page 60)* APRIL-DECEMBER

Poisonous species
Turban fungus *(page 178)* APRIL-MAY

Summer and autumn

For most fungi the underground mycelium is actively growing at this time but for others this is when the season begins. From mid-June onwards the boletes start to appear, soon followed by the chanterelles, brittle gills and milk caps.

Apple brittle gill *(page 90)* JULY-SEPTEMBER
Autumn chanterelle *(page 26)* SEPTEMBER-NOVEMBER
Bay bolete *(page 128)* AUGUST-NOVEMBER
Beefsteak fungus *(page 142)* JULY-OCTOBER
Blue-green funnel cap *(page 56)* AUGUST-OCTOBER
Blue-yellow brittle gill *(page 88)* JULY-NOVEMBER
Blusher *(page 102)* JUNE-OCTOBER (when cooked)
Brown birch rough stalk *(page 122)* JULY-OCTOBER
Buff meadow cap *(page 52)* SEPTEMBER-OCTOBER
Caesar's mushroom *(page 98)* JULY-OCTOBER (southern Europe only)
Cauliflower fungus *(page 144)* SEPTEMBER-OCTOBER
Chanterelle *(page 24)* JUNE-NOVEMBER
Common puffball *(page 114)* JULY-OCTOBER
Common yellow brittle gill *(page 84)* AUGUST-NOVEMBER
Cracked green brittle gill *(page 86)* JULY-OCTOBER
Deceiver *(page 58)* AUGUST-NOVEMBER
Field blewit *(page 80)* SEPTEMBER-NOVEMBER
Field mushroom *(page 36)* JULY-OCTOBER
Giant puffball *(page 112)* JULY-SEPTEMBER
Grisette *(page 184)* JUNE-NOVEMBER (edible when cooked)
Gypsy *(page 50)* AUGUST-OCTOBER (rare in Britain)

Poisonous species
Blusher *(page 182)* JUNE-OCTOBER (when raw)
Club-footed funnel cap *(page 196)* SEPTEMBER-NOVEMBER
Common earthball *(page 236)* JULY-OCTOBER
Common white fibre cap *(page 200)* JUNE-NOVEMBER
Copper trumpet *(page 206)* JULY-OCTOBER
Cream clot *(page 204)* AUGUST-NOVEMBER
Deadly Lepiota *(page 174)* AUGUST-OCTOBER *(Deadly)*
Death cap *(page 166)* AUGUST-SEPTEMBER *(Deadly)*
Destroying angel *(page 168)* AUGUST-SEPTEMBER *(Deadly)*
Devil's bolete *(page 234)* JULY-SEPTEMBER
Fly agaric *(page 212)* AUGUST-NOVEMBER
Foxy-orange web cap *(page 176)* SEPTEMBER-NOVEMBER
Girdled mottle gill *(page 190)* JULY-OCTOBER
Golden wax cap *(page 224)* JULY-NOVEMBER

Poisonous species

Common ink cap *(page 194)* JANUARY-DECEMBER
Red-staining fibre cap *(page 202)* MARCH-OCTOBER

Mushrooms which extend into winter are those which can survive the early frosts, such as the wood blewit, oyster mushrooms and jew's ear

Branched oyster mushroom *(page 134)* JUNE-DECEMBER
Fairy ring champignon *(page 72)* MARCH-NOVEMBER
Fawn shield cap *(page 62)* JANUARY-DECEMBER
Jew's ear *(page 158)* JANUARY-DECEMBER
Oyster mushroom *(page 132)* SEPTEMBER-MARCH
Périgord truffle *(page 150)* NOVEMBER-MARCH (southern Europe only)
Velvet shank *(page 46)* SEPTEMBER-MARCH
Wood blewit *(page 78)* SEPTEMBER-DECEMBER

Grisette *(page 184)* JUNE-NOVEMBER (when raw)
Liberty cap *(page 188)* JULY-NOVEMBER
Lilac bonnet cap *(page 208)* AUGUST-NOVEMBER
Liquorice milk cap *(page 226)* AUGUST-NOVEMBER
Livid pink gill *(page 220)* JULY-OCTOBER
Marginate pixy cap *(page 172)* SEPTEMBER-NOVEMBER
Orange scale head *(page 192)* AUGUST-DECEMBER
Panther *(page 214)* AUGUST-NOVEMBER
Peppery milk cap *(page 228)* AUGUST-NOVEMBER
Poison pie *(page 232)* AUGUST-NOVEMBER
Sickener *(page 230)* JULY-OCT
Spring Amanita *(page 170)* JUNE-SEPTEMBER (southern Europe only)
Tiger Knight cap *(page 222)* SEPTEMBER-OCTOBER
Yellow stainer *(page 218)* JUNE-OCTOBER

Hen of the woods *(page 138)* JULY-OCTOBER
Honey fungus *(page 44)* AUGUST-NOVEMBER
Horn of Plenty *(page 28)* AUGUST-NOVEMBER
Horse mushroom *(page 38)* AUGUST-OCTOBER
Jelly leaf *(page 160)* JUNE-DECEMBER
King oyster mushroom *(page 136)* JUNE-OCTOBER (southern Europe only)
Meadow puffball *(page 116)* JULY-OCTOBER
Miller *(page 54)* JULY-NOVEMBER
Orange birch rough stalk *(page 124)* JULY-OCTOBER
Orange-brown milk cap *(page 94)* AUGUST-OCTOBER
Parasol mushroom *(page 66)* JULY-OCTOBER
Penny bun bolete *(page 120)* AUGUST-NOVEMBER
Prince *(page 40)* AUGUST-OCTOBER
Saffron milk cap *(page 92)* AUGUST-OCTOBER
Scaly wood mushroom *(page 42)* AUGUST-OCTOBER
Shaggy parasol *(page 68)* JUNE-OCTOBER
Sheep polypore *(page 32)* AUGUST-NOVEMBER
Slippery Jack *(page 126)* SEPTEMBER-OCTOBER
Tawny grisette *(page 100)* JUNE-NOVEMBER (edible when cooked)
Wood urchin *(page 30)* AUGUST-NOVEMBER
WhitePiedmont truffle *(page 152)* AUGUST-SEPTEMBER

Hunting for edible mushrooms

Trampling is more damaging than over picking – but avoid both

Finding edible mushrooms cannot always be guaranteed: much depends on the time of year, the location, and the recent weather conditions. Generally, mushrooms, like all fungi, require water in order to grow, so a wet autumn weekend is likely to prove the most profitable. Hot, dry summer days may be less rewarding. It is often wise to choose an area where there is some variation in the vegetation, such as a conifer wood as well as leafy woodland, with perhaps some grassland nearby. Try a little adventurous searching over the course of a season, and you will probably discover some worthwhile collecting areas. Once such a site is found, it often remains a closely guarded secret with the discoverer. Remember always to observe the Country Code, and the laws of trespass (page 253). Seeking the landowner's permission is often rewarding and can save a good deal of embarrassment or worse.

The experienced mushroom hunter is well prepared. It is useful to take a sharp knife for removing fruitbodies growing on wood, or for slicing them open to check for maggots. A flat-bottomed wickerwork basket, large enough to prevent fruitbodies from becoming crushed, is very useful; so is a notebook to deal with any uncertain species, recording the surrounding trees, the smell of the fresh fruitbody, and any changes in flesh colour. (A pencil is better than a pen in wet weather). A numbering system is helpful for easy reference. A hand-lens (x10) is invaluable for recording details, such as the cap surface structure, the attachment of the gills to the stem and similar structures. It is useful to take along a small field guide, not only for the recognition of the mushrooms but also for determining the trees and surrounding vegetation. Be well prepared for wet weather in the autumn. It is all too easy to get lost in an unfamiliar area when collecting as the eyes are mostly concentrated on the ground, especially under trees – so a map and compass might come in useful.

Picking mushrooms does no harm to the fungus, which is mostly underground, but avoid overpicking. On the other hand, a range of fruitbodies, from the young, primordial stage to the fully mature form may be necessary to clinch identification. Excessive trampling and digging up the soil, or the unnecessary moving of fallen logs and branches can also be harmful. Only pick specimens in sound condition, remove the mushroom gently and ensure that you include the base of the stem. Look out for the presence of the cup-like volva at the stem base of the poisonous *Amanita* species. Equally, the absence of a volva or scales at the stem base can prove an essential clue. Each collection should be kept separate, and wrapping in waxed paper will keep them fresh; polythene bags are not generally recommended, as the fruitbodies will 'sweat' and are easily squashed. Limit yourself to just a few species until you become more expert. It is always a good idea for the beginner to be accompanied by someone who is knowledgeable on mushrooms – it is the easiest and quickest way to learn what to look for and what to avoid.

On returning home, get the identification guide out straight away – figuring out unfamiliar species is easiest while the fruitbody is still fresh. It may be necessary to take a 'spore-print' – the spore colour deposit can often clinch identification. Place a cap, with the stem removed, on a sheet of paper, cover with a tin or jam-jar to prevent desiccation, put in a cool place and leave for a few hours. Spores will be released by the gills and drop to the paper. Remember mushrooms soon deteriorate.

If you are in any doubt over the identity of a mushroom, then do not eat it. Mycophagy, or mushroom eating, is not a time for Russian roulette: poisonous species can be deadly, even in small amounts.

Classifying fungi

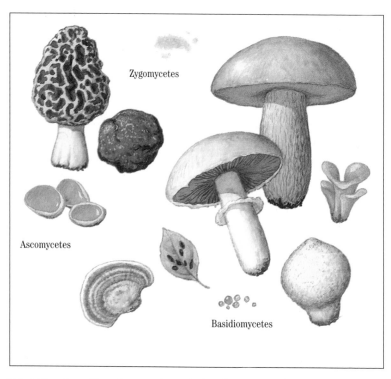

Zygomycetes

Ascomycetes

Basidiomycetes

The Kingdom Fungi comprises three classes:
- Ascomycetes (largest order, cup fungi, flask fungi, truffles.
- Basidiomycetes (mushrooms, brackets, puffballs, jelly fungi).
- Zygomycetes (includes the pin moulds).

There are more than 450 families of fungus worldwide, containing 6,000 genera and an estimated 1,600,000 species. All three classes can have complicated life cycles, in which each species can exist in two or more states. There is a sexually produced state (the teleomorph) producing spores through a process of the cell nuclei fusing and dividing (meiosis), and an asexual state (the anamorph), with non-sexually formed spores, the conidiospores. Often the asexual state lives independently of the sexual state, and has been given a different name. These are sometimes placed in a fourth, artificial class, the Deuteromycetes (or *Fungi Imperfecti*). Slowly scientists are learning which asexual state belongs to which sexual state; the two states are collectively referred to as the holomorph. The slime moulds, water moulds and chytrids are not true fungi, but are often classed as such.

A SIMPLIFIED CLASSIFICATION OF FUNGI

1 Kingdom FUNGI

(Chitinous hyphae; no flagellate states). 'Flagellate' means with a flagellum or whiplash tail like a tadpole.

Class 1
  ASCOMYCETES (largest; meiospores in asci)
  cup fungi, morels, truffles (45 families), flask fungi (64 families).

Class 2
  BASIDIOMYCETES (meiospores on basidia)
  Subclass Holobasidiomycetidae
  Order 1 Cantharellales (12 families, chanterelles, tooth fungi).
  Order 2 Agaricales (24 families, mushrooms and toadstools).
  Order 3 Boletales (11 families, boletes).
  Order 4 Russulales (2 families, brittle gills and milk caps).
  Order 5 Poriales (12 families, bracket fungi).
  Order 6 Lycoperdales (10 families, puffballs, earthballs).
  Subclass Phragmobasidiomycetidae
  Orders 1-2 Tremellales and Auriculariales (18 families, jelly fungi).
  Order 3 Uredinales (15 families, rust fungi).
  Order 4 Ustilaginales (5 families, smut fungi).

Class ZYGOMYCETES (with meiosporic zygospores)
  Order 1 Mucorales (pin moulds).
  Order 2 Endogonales (pea truffles).

2 Kingdom PROTOCTISTA

(Flagellate states present)

Class **MYXOMYCETES** (slime moulds).

Class **OOMYCETES** (water moulds).

Class **CHYTRIDIOMYCETES** (chytrids – microscopic aquatic fungi).

Identifying edible fungi

**An instant key to the identification of the main
groups of edible and poisonous mushrooms**

1

Fruitbody bracket- or shelf-like; no gills on underside of cap ⟹ **2**

Fruitbody with short, hollow stem; head with honeycomb ridges or brain-shaped ⟹ **morels** (*page 146*); **turban fungus** (*page 178*)

Fruitbody without a stem ⟹ **4**

Fruitbody with a cap with radiating gills, ridges or spines on the underside ⟹ **5**

2

Pores on underside of cap ⟹ **3**

No pores under cap; fruitbody gelatinous ⟹ **jelly fungi** (*page 156*)

3

Flesh firm to hard, long-lived; growing on wood ⟹ **bracket fungi** (*page 130*)

Flesh soft, short-lived, growing on the ground ⟹ **boletes** (*pages 118, 234*)

4

Fruitbody small, cup- or saucer-shaped ⟹ **cup fungi** (*page 146*)

Fruitbody ball-shaped or with short stalk; becoming powdery ⟹ **puffballs** (*page 110*); **earthballs** (*page 236*)

Fruitbody ball-shaped; growing underground ⟹ **truffles** (*page 146*)

5

Fruitbody with a stem ⟹ **6**

Fruitbody without a stem or stem very reduced; laterally attached to wood ⟹ **oysters** (*page 130*)

6

Cap with thick ridges, wrinkling or spines, instead of gills, on underside ||||▶ **chanterelles** (*page 22*)

Cap with true gills ||||▶ **7**

7

Spore deposit blackish brown to black ||||▶ **true mushrooms** (*pages 36-43, 218*); **ink caps** (*page 104*); **liberty cap** (*page 188*); **mottle gills** (*page 190*); **sulphur tuft** (*page 61*)

Spore deposit rusty brown to dark brown; stem often with ring or cortina ||||▶ **web caps** (*pages 176, 233*); **fibre caps** (*pages 200-203*); **southern poplar mushroom** (*page 48*); **gypsy** (*page 50*); **two-toned scale head** (*page 60*)

Spore deposit pale pink to deep salmon pink ||||▶ **pink gills** (*page 220*); **shield caps** (*page 62*); **miller** (*page 54*); **blewits** (*page 76*)

Spore deposit white to yellowish ||||▶ **8**

8

Stem with a ring and/or a volva ||||▶ **Amanita** (*pages 96, 166-171*); **parasols** (*page 64*); **Lepiota** (*page 174*); **honey fungus** (*page 44*)

Stem without a ring or volva ||||▶ **9**

9

Fruitbodies forming fairy rings in grassland ||||▶ **fairy ring champignon** and **St. George's mushroom** (*page 70*)

Flesh crumbly; with or without latex ||||▶ **brittle gills and milk caps** (*pages 82, 226-231*)

Flesh soft fleshy but not crumbly; no latex ||||▶ **10**

10

Fruitbody growing on wood, tufted ||||▶ **velvet shank** (*page 46*); **copper trumpet** (*page 206*)

Fruitbody growing on the ground ||||▶ **funnel caps** (*pages 56, 196, 205*); **wax caps** (*pages 52, 224*); **knight caps** (*page 222*); **deceiver** (*page 58*)

Edible species: a top 20

Which are the best edible mushrooms? Well, of course, no two people would ever agree. On the other hand, it's harmless fun to try to list the most sought-after. In doing so, it seems fair to take into account relative ease of recognition; frequency of occurrence; and regional variation.

A comparison of an early French list (1947) with a recent British list (1990) shows remarkable differences. The French place the St. George's mushroom at the top followed by Caesar's mushroom and the common morel, with the Périgord truffle at number 10, the chanterelle at number 20 and the saffron milk cap down to number 43. In the British list, the first three are the penny bun bolete, parasol mushroom and the field mushroom, with morel down to number 12 and the St. George's mushroom at number 19. In both lists the milk caps and brittle gills scarcely appear, with the exception of the blue-yellow brittle gill. In eastern Scandinavia and Russia, however, the brittle gills and milk caps are particularly prized, especially the northern milk cap (page 95), woolly milk cap (page 93), ugly milk cap (page 227), and the rufous milk cap (page 227). In western Europe the latter two are deemed so unpalatable as to be included amongst the poisonous species. In France, Poland, Russia and Switzerland, dried and pickled mushrooms are an important export, and the ease of preservation of certain species, such as the fairy ring champignon, increases their popularity.

An overall survey might suggest the following to be the most desirable edible mushrooms in Europe, the first three confined to the Mediterranean countries, with the white Piedmont truffle earning the title of the world's most expensive food:

White piedmont truffle

Chanterelles and tooth fungi

The chanterelles are amongst the first to be sought after by the amateur collector, rivalling the *cep (Boletus edulis)*, and almost every country has its own popular name for chanterelles.

They are generally conspicuous, with striking colours, often bright orange or yellow, and easily spotted on the woodland floor. Strictly speaking, chanterelles are not true mushrooms, although superficially they bear a strong resemblance, with a fruitbody

Chanterelle

consisting of a cap, stem and gill-like structures. The latter, however, are not really gills but comprise thick, blunt, often branching ridges which run down the underside of the cap. The gills of a true mushroom have a thin, sharp edge.

There are numerous species of chanterelle, but first and foremost is the **chanterelle** itself (*Cantharellus cibarius*, page 24), also familiarly known as the *girolle* in French or *Pfifferling* in German. It appears in woodland, usually oak or beech, but also under conifers, such as spruce and pine. It is one of the mycorrhizal mushrooms, (forming an independent relationship with certain trees) and nobody has ever succeeded in its commercial cultivation. Chanterelles are widely available in shops and market places throughout Europe. In some countries, chanterelles are harvested on a commercial scale, with a tendency drastically to overpick the fruitbodies, so that the species have become less plentiful than they once were.

The chanterelle is a fast-growing mushroom. It is firm when it is dry, but does have a high water content and becomes waterlogged in wet weather. These mushrooms also dry well for later use, even retaining their scent of apricots.

Another species, considered by many to be superior in flavour to the chanterelle, is the **autumn chanterelle** (*Cantharellus tubiformis,* page 26), sometimes called the trumpet chanterelle. This is picked on a considerable scale, often commercially, throughout Scandinavia. It is able to withstand the early frosts and so remains plentiful throughout the late autumn season. Although it is likely to be present in enormous numbers, it may be difficult to find initially because the fruit-bodies blend with the fallen autumn leaves. Some people are allergic to this species, so it is advisable to eat only a small portion when trying it for the first time.

The **horn of plenty** (*Craterellus cornucopioides*, page 28) is another related species which can be difficult to find owing to its dark, greyish colours. This differs from most chanterelles in having a tall, slender fruitbody which is hollow, virtually lacking any stem, and resembling a slender vase, without any gills or ridges. It is a good, edible mushroom, so do not be put off by the names it has earned because of its dark colours – *trompe des mortes* and 'black trumpet'. It can be dried and is very good in stews.

Worth mentioning here are the rare **vase fungi** (*Gomphus* species), which resemble chanterelles in having similar, blunt ridges on the underside of the cap. They can be recognized by their brown spore deposit.

The **wood urchin** (*Hydnum repandum*, page 30) is related to the chanterelle but differs in having small spines or teeth instead of ridges on the underside of the cap. It is often placed in a group collectively referred to as the **tooth fungi**, by virtue of their spines, but the other species in the group are not closely related or considered edible. The wood urchin is also known as the 'hedgehog fungus', the 'wood hedgehog', or 'sweet tooth' and is sold in supermarkets under the name *pied de mouton*. These are firm, fleshy and popular mushrooms.

Unrelated, but also edible, are the **spine fungi** (*Hericium* species), including the **coral spine fungus** (*Hericium coralloides*) and the **lion's mane** (*Hericium erinaceum*). These mushrooms are white, grow tufted on wood often high up on the tree and never on the ground, and consist almost entirely of spines. The lion's mane is a highly prized mushroom in China where it is called the 'monkey head', and reputed to have many health-giving qualities.

The closely related **sheep polypore** (*Albatrellus ovinus,* page 32) is one of the few edible, bracket fungi in Europe.

Chanterelle

Cantharellus cibarius

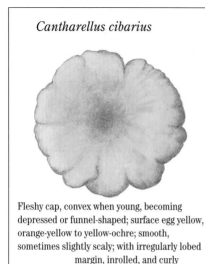

All parts yellow; thick, forking, decurrent ridges; white spore deposit

Fleshy cap, convex when young, becoming depressed or funnel-shaped; surface egg yellow, orange-yellow to yellow-ochre; smooth, sometimes slightly scaly; with irregularly lobed margin, inrolled, and curly

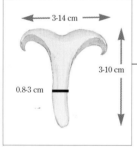

Spore print

Ridges deeply decurrent and gill-like, thick and narrow, often forked and interveined; egg yellow

Stem generally short, more or less cylindrical, tapering below and merging with the pileus above. Same colour as pileus, smooth

3-14 cm

3-10 cm

0.8-3 cm

Flesh up to 1.5 cm thick, fleshy-fibrous, whitish to yellowish, drying paler; smells pleasantly of dried apricots

Frequency common throughout Europe

Spore deposit pale pinkish yellow

A conspicuous, common and widespread mushroom. Long considered one of *the* edible mushrooms, it appears in the earliest herbals and is popular in 'French cuisine'. It needs plenty of rain and prefers acid soils; it forms associations with the roots of many forest trees, and cannot easily be cultivated, so is largely harvested in the wild. The pale chanterelle (*Cantharellus pallens*) has a white to pale yellow cap and is much rarer; the orange chanterelle (*Cantharellus friesii*) is orange to pinkish orange, with pink ridges.

EATING

A mild but aromatic taste. Its firm texture and delicate flavour require slow, gentle cooking. Rather dry and tough by nature, the chanterelle requires a considerable quantity of fluid for proper cooking. All parts are delicious.

Habitat
On the ground in moist, broadleaved and coniferous woodland, often by the edge of paths; considered to have a broad host range, and is found among oak, beech, birch, spruce and pine

LOOKALIKES

False chanterelle *Hygrophoropsis aurantiaca* Very common in conifer woods, this is the species most often confused with the chanterelle. Pale yellow to orange but with true, thin gills which repeatedly fork. Rarely causing stomach upset, although generally not poisonous, but worthless.

False chanterelle

Foxy-orange cortinarius *Cortinarius speciosissimus* and related species. Commonest in southern Europe, rare in the north, growing on the ground in conifer woods. Contains the deadly orellanin, which causes kidney failure. Uniformly yellowish to reddish brown, with thin, unbranched gills which finally turn brown. The spore deposit is brown. *See page 176.*

Foxy-orange cortinarius

Copper trumpet *Omphalotus olearius* Uniformly yellowish to reddish brown; more common in southern Europe and rare in Britain; always growing in clusters at base of trunks and buried roots, especially of olive trees, but also oak and elm. Can cause severe stomach upsets. *See page 206.*

Autumn chanterelle

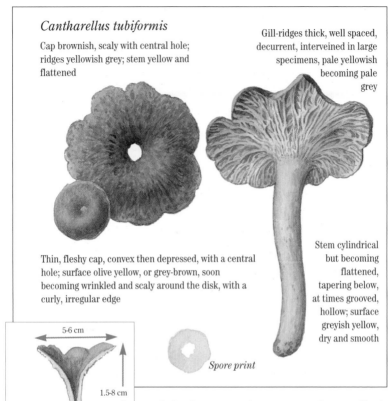

Cantharellus tubiformis

Cap brownish, scaly with central hole; ridges yellowish grey; stem yellow and flattened

Gill-ridges thick, well spaced, decurrent, interveined in large specimens, pale yellowish becoming pale grey

Thin, fleshy cap, convex then depressed, with a central hole; surface olive yellow, or grey-brown, soon becoming wrinkled and scaly around the disk, with a curly, irregular edge

Stem cylindrical but becoming flattened, tapering below, at times grooved, hollow; surface greyish yellow, dry and smooth

5-6 cm

1.5-8 cm

0.3-1 cm

Spore print

Flesh thin, whitish to yellow-brown, with a pleasant smell

Frequency very common in northern localities

Spore deposit creamish white to pale lemon yellow

Also known as the trumpet chanterelle, it can grow in very large numbers covering a wide area of woodland. Unlike related species, it survives early frosts, so is collected on a commercial basis in Scandinavia. Some consider it better to eat than the chanterelle. Can be difficult to find as the fruitbodies blend with fallen, withered leaves. Take care when eating this for the first time – some people are allergic to it.

Cantharellus tubiformis var. *lutescens* has a pale yellow cap, ridges and stem.

EATING

All parts are good, with a mild taste. Fruitbodies may be dried to preserve them.

Habitat
In troops in both coniferous and leafy woods; prefers boggy areas in northern localities

LOOKALIKES

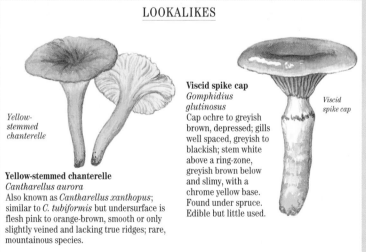

Yellow-stemmed chanterelle

Yellow-stemmed chanterelle
Cantharellus aurora
Also known as *Cantharellus xanthopus*;
similar to *C. tubiformis* but undersurface is
flesh pink to orange-brown, smooth or only
slightly veined and lacking true ridges; rare,
mountainous species.

Viscid spike cap
*Gomphidius
glutinosus*
Cap ochre to greyish
brown, depressed; gills
well spaced, greyish to
blackish; stem white
above a ring-zone,
greyish brown below
and slimy, with a
chrome yellow base.
Found under spruce.
Edible but little used.

*Viscid
spike cap*

Horn of plenty

Craterellus cornucopioides

Tall, high, hollow, funnel shape; dull grey to blackish colour, paler in dry conditions, tufted; outer surface smooth without gills

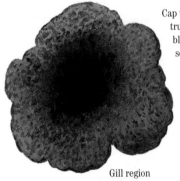

Cap tall, deeply funnel-shaped to trumpet-shaped; surface black to blackish-brown, drying greyish brown, scurfy to felty, often with a curled, undulating, down-curved edge

Spore print

Gill region smooth to slightly veined and wrinkled, pale brown to grey-brown

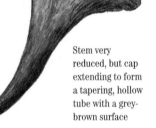

Stem very reduced, but cap extending to form a tapering, hollow tube with a grey-brown surface

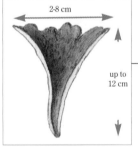

2-8 cm

up to 12 cm

Flesh thin, up to 1 mm thick, soft-leathery, grey; has a pleasant smell

Frequency locally common and abundant

Spore deposit off-white

The horn of plenty is a good, edible species, although its dark colour has earned it the rather sinister names of 'trompette des mortes' (trumpet of the dead) and 'black trumpet'. In France, it is known as 'la viande des pauvres' (poor man's meat). The mushroom can be dried and preserved for use in stews. It is distinctly vase- or trumpet-shaped and hollow with very little true stem. It usually grows in large troops amongst leaf litter but its dark colour can make it difficult to find.

EATING

A strongly flavoured, aromatic mushroom, rarely requiring additional seasoning. Remove solid base, slice and gently clean.

Habitat
Clustered, in both deciduous and coniferous woodland, but especially common in woodlands of hazel, beech and oak; also grows in mossy pine woods

LOOKALIKES

Grey chanterelle

Grey chanterelle
Pseudocraterellus cinereus
Entire fruitbody greyish brown to black, with a funnel-shaped cap, 2-6 cm across, but strong branching ridges on the undersurface; has a true stem; lacks the fragrant, fruity odour and is less tasty. Never abundant and not considered edible.

Blackening brittle gill
Russula nigricans
Cap very large, 10-20 cm across, at first white soon grey-brown to black, with thick, white, brittle gills which finally blacken; stem well-developed, blackening. Edible with a peppery taste, but not recommended.

Blackening brittle gill

29

Wood urchin

Hydnum repandum

Fruitbody firm fleshy, whitish to pinkish buff; lower surface covered with numerous, fine spines, short stocky stem

Cap at first convex, variable, cushion-shaped to depressed; surface white to pale pinkish buff, velvety to felty becoming smooth and shiny when dry, not zoned; margin entire, thick, persistently inrolled

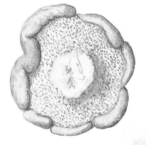

Spines adnate, at times subdecurrent at least down one side of the stem, white or with a pinkish tint; individual spines soft and brittle, fragile, uneven in length, 4-8 mm long, very crowded

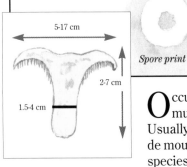

Stem central but mostly excentric, fairly stocky, cylindrical or swollen below; solid; surface whitish, paler than pileus, covered with fine hairs, becoming smooth, arising from a mass of fungal threads

5-17 cm

2-7 cm

1.5-4 cm

Spore print

Flesh thick, soft and fleshy, white; may discolour reddish when bruised; smell pleasant but faint

Frequency locally common, throughout Europe

Spore deposit pale cream

Occurring alone or in small groups, this mushroom is not likely to be confused. Usually sold under the French name 'pied de mouton' (sheep's foot), it is a firm, fleshy species which is good to eat. Occasionally, a pure white form is found, which tends to be more robust and of firmer texture.

The reddish wood urchin (*Hydnum rufescens*) is smaller and more slender, with an ochraceous- to brownish-orange cap. The stem is typically central, and the spines are not decurrent on the stem.

EATING

A pleasant, mild yet delicate flavour. Take care not to over-season. Best when simply sautéed.

Habitat
Amongst humus
in deciduous
woods,
especially oak,
beech and birch
where it can be
abundant, but
also found in
pine and spruce
woodland

LOOKALIKES

Chanterelle

Scaly tooth

Scaly tooth
Sarcodon imbricatus Easily
distinguished by the
yellowish brown cap with
rings of coarse scales. Thick
stem is brownish and the
spines soon become brown.
Widespread but rare, in
coniferous woods. Inedible
and worthless.

Chanterelle
Cantharellus cibarius
Although differing in
structure, this is closely
related and superficially
similar to the wood urchin.
See page 24.

Strongly scented spine fungus
Phellodon confluens Caps
normally fusing to form
compound fruitbodies, at
first white becoming
brownish, with pale greyish
spines. On the ground in leafy
woods, such as beech, chestnut
and oak. Widespread but
uncommon. Inedible.

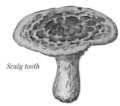

Strongly scented spine fungus

Sheep polypore

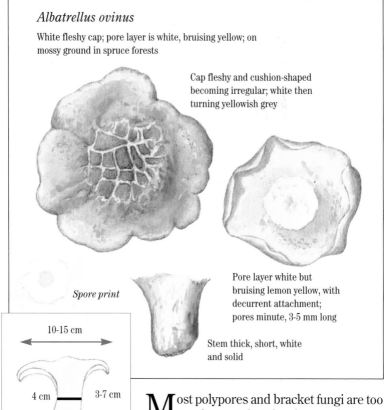

Albatrellus ovinus

White fleshy cap; pore layer is white, bruising yellow; on mossy ground in spruce forests

Cap fleshy and cushion-shaped becoming irregular; white then turning yellowish grey

Spore print

Pore layer white but bruising lemon yellow, with decurrent attachment; pores minute, 3-5 mm long

Stem thick, short, white and solid

10-15 cm

4 cm   3-7 cm

Flesh up to 2 cm thick, white, with an aromatic smell

Frequency widespread in Scandinavia, north and central Europe wherever there are spruce forests, but absent in western Europe

Spore deposit white

Most polypores and bracket fungi are too tough to eat, but the sheep polypore is truly edible. It grows on the ground, has a soft, crumbly flesh, and is often collected in large quantities.

The small fruitbodies can look remarkably like those of the wood urchin. The difference is that the sheep polypore has a pore layer instead of spines on the underside. It might also be confused with some of the boletes, but differs in having a tube layer which is not easily separable from the flesh.

EATING

✗✗

Good to eat, with a mild taste. When cooked, the flesh turns a yellowish colour.

Habitat
In troops on the
ground in
conifer woods,
especially
spruce

LOOKALIKES

Bread polypore

Bread polypore *Albatrellus cristatus*
Similar to the sheep polypore but growing
in small groups with overlapping caps,
which are pale yellowish brown. The white
pores bruise reddish, and the stem is more
slender. Edible, but not recommended.
Found in spruce and pine woods but
absent from Britain and the Atlantic coast
of Europe.

Wood urchin
Hydnum repandum Remarkably similar
to the sheep polypore but underside of cap
covered with numerous small spines.
Widespread, including Britain.
See page 30.

Mushrooms and toadstools

Although the terms 'mushroom' and 'toadstool' are familiar in the English language, their origins, meanings and distinctions remain obscure. Much has been written about the word mushroom, and it is known to date back to at least Old French and Old English. The usually held derivation is from the French word, *mousseron*, referring to moss, but this is disputed. The meaning of toadstool might seem self-evident and there has been a long association for many centuries between toadstools and toads (or frogs). Both were regarded as poisonous and therefore despised.

Field mushroom.

The true mushrooms, which include the familiar, white **cultivated mushroom** (*Agaricus bisporus,* page 37) belong to one genus, namely *Agaricus.* In Europe, there are more than 50 species of *Agaricus,* most of these are edible. Perhaps the best known is the **field mushroom** (*Agaricus campestris,* page 36), which is commonly found in fields and open grassland, particularly during damp early autumns, and the one most often illustrated in school biology textbooks. The **horse mushroom** (*Agaricus arvensis,* page 38) is equally common in similar situations and can form large fairy rings.

Not all species called mushroom belong to the genus *Agaricus.* A good example is the **southern poplar mushroom** (*Agrocybe cylindrica*), also known as the **black poplar mushroom** (*Agrocybe aegerita*). It forms dense clusters at the base of stumps and old trunks of

Horse mushroom

leafy trees. In Mediterranean countries, this edible mushroom is semi-cultivated. A white-spored species but with an ubiquitous distribution is the **honey fungus** (*Armillaria mellea,* page 44). This may be found growing in large tufts on stumps and amongst tree roots throughout the late autumn.

Honey fungus

Brightly coloured mushrooms and toadstools often cause alarm and are considered as species to avoid. This is not always the case, however: the **blue-green funnel cap** (*Clitocybe odora,* page 56), the russet-coloured **deceiver** (*Laccaria laccata,* page 58) and its relative, the **amethyst deceiver** (*Laccaria amethystina,* page 59) are all edible. Similarly, mushrooms with pink spore deposits include many poisonous species, but two exceptions are the white **miller** (*Clitopilus prunulus,* page 54) and the **fawn shield cap** (*Pluteus cervinus,* page 62).

Many of the mushrooms and toadstools with brown or blackish brown gills and spore deposits are poisonous and should definitely be avoided. The several hundred species of web caps (*Cortinarius* species) and fibre caps (*Inocybe* species) fall into this category. Exceptions to the rule include the **gypsy** (*Rozites caperata,* page 101) and the **wine cap** (*Stropharia rugoso-annulata,* page 51). Both species bear a conspicuous membranous ring on the stem, separating them from the many inedible and sometimes poisonous web caps.

Gypsy

Wine cap

Field mushroom

Agaricus campestris

Grassland species; pink gills turning chocolate brown, small
ring on stem; flesh discolours pink, no yellow bruising

Cap strongly convex, becoming almost
flattened, pure white or sometimes with
greyish-brown tints at the centre; dry, smooth
or indistinctly scaly in old specimens

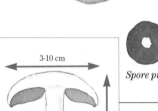

Gills free,
bright pink
becoming dark
chocolate brown,
broad and crowded

Stem short and
cylindrical or
tapering at the
base; white,
smooth, bearing a
small, thin ring
which quickly
disappears on
weathering

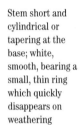

Spore print

3-10 cm

3-6 cm

1-1.5 cm

Flesh thick, white, quickly
discolouring pinkish when
broken open; smell pleasant

Frequency common

Spore deposit blackish brown

The best-known mushroom, the field
mushroom, is familiar to most people as
it is the one usually illustrated in biology
textbooks. It has a pleasant odour, and is
said to have a nuttier flavour than the commercial 'cultivated mushroom'. It can be
identified by the reddening flesh, and the
small, simple ring on the stem.

The horse mushroom (*A. arvensis*),
(page 38), occurs in similar situations but
bruises yellow, and the cultivated mushroom (*A. bisporus*) has a much larger ring.

EATING

✗ ✗ ✗

Good, edible mushroom with a nutty taste.

Habitat
scattered in
open grassland

LOOKALIKES

*Cultivated
mushroom*

**Cultivated
mushroom**
*Agaricus
bisporus*
The pure
white form is
mostly grown
commercially, but in
the wild this
uncommon species
typically has brown,
fibrous scales on the
cap. Otherwise differs from the field
mushroom in the much larger, less
ephemeral ring, and the flesh not reddening
so quickly.

Yellow stainer
Agaricus xanthoderma Easily mistaken for
the field mushroom or the horse mushroom,
but the surface
stains bright
yellow, and is
especially yellow
in the flesh at the stem
base. Also has a large,
membranous ring, and
an unpleasant smell. One
of the few poisonous
Agaricus species. *See
page 218.*

*Yellow
stainer*

Wood mushroom
Agaricus silvicola A
white to cream mushroom
with a smooth cap, a swollen
stem base and a thin ring; bruises yellow and
has a smell of aniseed. Found in woodland,
not grassland. Edible, but do not confuse
with the deadly destroying angel.

Horse mushroom

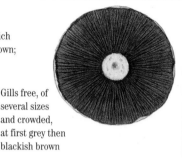

Agaricus arvensis

Large and fleshy, white cap and stem which bruise yellowish; gills grey to blackish brown; stem with a large ring

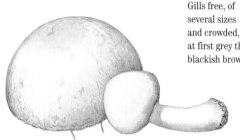

Gills free, of several sizes and crowded, at first grey then blackish brown

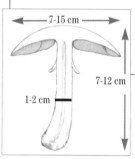

Cap strongly rounded at first but expanding and becoming flattened and plate-like, with a white surface bruising yellowish brown; smooth or with small scales towards edge

Spore print

Stem smooth and white but bruising yellowish brown, with a large, hanging, membranous, white ring towards the top, with cogwheel-like scales on the underside

7-15 cm

7-12 cm

1-2 cm

Flesh thick and firm, white and not turning yellow in the stem, with a distinctive smell of bitter almonds

Frequency commonly found, often forming large fairy rings

Spore deposit blackish brown

The name 'horse' has nothing to do with the animal: it is an old term indicating the large size, especially when the caps have fully expanded. These mushrooms are often more common than the field mushroom (page 36). The white surfaces gradually discolour yellowish brown as the horse mushroom matures.

You should take great care to avoid confusing this mushroom with the yellow stainer which can cause unpleasant poisoning (page 218).

EATING	A true mushroom flavour, rather nutty; the firm white flesh of older specimens soon develops maggots.

Habitat
In fields and pastures during the autumn

LOOKALIKES

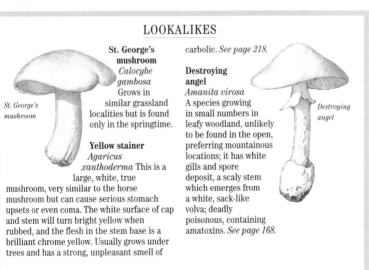

St. George's mushroom

St. George's mushroom
Calocybe gambosa
Grows in similar grassland localities but is found only in the springtime.

Yellow stainer
Agaricus xanthoderma This is a large, white, true mushroom, very similar to the horse mushroom but can cause serious stomach upsets or even coma. The white surface of cap and stem will turn bright yellow when rubbed, and the flesh in the stem base is a brilliant chrome yellow. Usually grows under trees and has a strong, unpleasant smell of carbolic. *See page 218.*

Destroying angel
Amanita virosa
A species growing in small numbers in leafy woodland, unlikely to be found in the open, preferring mountainous locations; it has white gills and spore deposit, a scaly stem which emerges from a white, sack-like volva; deadly poisonous, containing amatoxins. *See page 168.*

Destroying angel

The prince

Agaricus augustus

Large size, yellowy scaly cap, pinkish to blackish brown gill, tall stem with large ring; yellow bruising

Cap almost round, then expanding to convex, but retaining a flattened top, covered with small, tawny brown, fibrous scales in concentric rings on a cream yellow background, bruising deep yellow

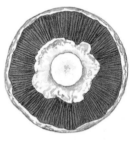

Spore print

Ring large, membranous, white, smooth above and scaly on underside

Gills free, pinkish to blackish brown, crowded

Stem tall, cylindrical, thicker towards the base; white, bruising yellow, smooth above the ring; soft and scaly below the ring

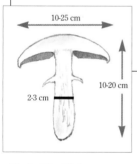

10-25 cm

10-20 cm

2-3 cm

Flesh white, thick, not reddening, with a smell of bitter almonds

Frequency uncommon

Spore deposit brownish black

One of the largest true mushrooms, and among the best of the edible species, but it is only occasionally found and rarely in large quantities. As it is a yellowing species be sure to avoid confusion with the yellow stáiner. Sometimes attributed to the Emperor Augustus but unlikely to have been eaten by the Romans, and the epithet probably refers to the Latin word for majestic.

The scaly wood mushroom (page 42), is similar but smaller, and the flesh quickly discolours red when broken open.

EATING

Excellent; all parts edible, with nutty taste.

Habitat
In small groups, rarely solitary, in either coniferous woods, especially spruce, or in parks under leafy trees

LOOKALIKES

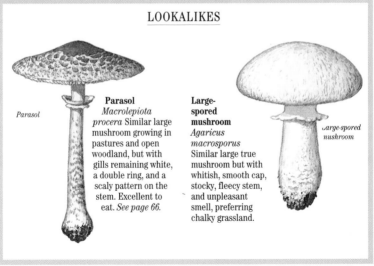

Parasol

Parasol
Macrolepiota procera Similar large mushroom growing in pastures and open woodland, but with gills remaining white, a double ring, and a scaly pattern on the stem. Excellent to eat. *See page 66.*

Large-spored mushroom
Agaricus macrosporus Similar large true mushroom but with whitish, smooth cap, stocky, fleecy stem, and unpleasant smell, preferring chalky grassland.

Large-spored mushroom

Scaly wood mushroom

Agaricus silvaticus

Scaly grey-brown cap, flesh becoming blood red; large ring, in conifer woods, gills dark brown

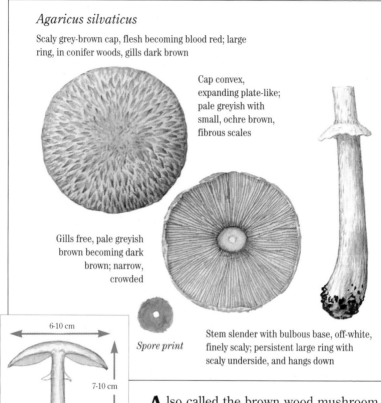

Cap convex, expanding plate-like; pale greyish with small, ochre brown, fibrous scales

Gills free, pale greyish brown becoming dark brown; narrow, crowded

Spore print

Stem slender with bulbous base, off-white, finely scaly; persistent large ring with scaly underside, and hangs down

6-10 cm

7-10 cm

1-1.5 cm

Flesh fairly thin, white becoming deep blood red when exposed, eventually brownish, with pleasant smell

Frequency locally abundant

Spore deposit dark brown

Also called the brown wood mushroom, the scaly wood mushroom is very common in conifer woods where it grows in clusters. It is one of the smaller edible species and belongs to a group of scaly true mushrooms that bruise reddish in young specimens. Do not be discouraged by the deep blood-red flesh. Of the sixty or so true mushroom species in Europe, about half (including the cultivated mushroom and the field mushroom) have red-bruising flesh; the remainder have a yellow-staining surface.

EATING

Good, with a mild taste, but usually attacked by insect larvae.

Habitat
Conifer woods, especially under pines, preferring chalky ground

LOOKALIKES

Flat-topped mushroom
Agaricus praeclaresquamosus
Also known as *Agaricus meleagris* and *Agaricus placomyces*. Cap with greyish scales and centre black, bruising bright yellow. Flesh yellowing especially at stipe base. Unpleasant smell of iodoform. Closely related to the yellow stainer, and therefore poisonous.

Flat-topped mushroom

Great wood mushroom
Agaricus haemorrhoidarius Very similar but found in leafy woodland and somewhat larger with a stouter stem. The flesh reddens deeply. Infrequent, usually at the edge of woods and coppices.

Great wood mushroom

Shaggy parasol
Macrolepiota rhacodes Found under shrubs and on compost heaps. Scaly cap, white stem bruising brown, with swollen base, and large ring. Gills remaining whitish. *See page 68*

Honey fungus

Armillaria mellea

Dense clusters at tree bases; yellow-brown caps, pale decurrent gills, large ring on stem; black threads under bark

Gills shortly decurrent, whitish but developing reddish stains, narrow and moderately crowded

Cap convex to flattened with a wavy margin; yellow-brown or honey colour to pinkish brown, with tiny, scattered, dark brown, hair-like scales, sticky to the touch when young and fresh

Stem cylindrical, soon hollow, whitish becoming rusty brown, fibrous, with a thick, cottony ring attached to the upper region; the stem is attached at the base to thick, black, coarse threads which branch and spread over the host plant and through the soil

Spore print

3-12 cm

5-15 cm

1-2 cm

Flesh white, firm, with an indistinct smell of mushroom

Frequency very common in late autumn

Spore deposit cream

A common, fleshy mushroom, it grows in large tufts on stumps and amongst tree roots in late autumn; often abundant but can be variable in colour. It may attack garden trees and shrubs. Underneath the bark of the tree you can usually find strands resembling black, flat strands of mycelium; these explain the alternative name of 'boot-lace fungus'. Although frequently eaten, some care needs to be taken. The fruitbodies should always be cooked, and it is best to eat only the very young specimens.

EATING	Caps edible when young and fresh. It is advisable to sample only a small portion when eating for the first time, taking only the youngest fruitbodies. Older fruitbodies develop a bitter taste, and can cause stomach upsets in some people.

Habitat
Clustered on roots and stumps of many deciduous trees

LOOKALIKES

Ringless honey fungus
Armillaria tabescens Very similar but the cap is dry and the stem lacks a ring. Cap yellowish brown to tawny brown, with small, rusty brown scales of fine fibres towards disk; stem tapering below, whitish, bruising brown; usually found on wood of deciduous trees; western Europe but not in Scandinavia.

Ringless honey fungus

Two-toned scale head
Kuehneromyces mutabilis Clustered on old stumps and dead tree bases throughout summer and autumn. Recognized by the brown, two-tone cap and dark brown, scaly stem with a small ring. *See page 60.*

Two-toned scale head

Sulphur tuft
Hypholoma fasciculare Fruitbody uniformly sulphur yellow, but adnate gills finally purplish black. Stem yellowish, with a ring-like zone of dark brown fibres. Can cause severe gastric upsets. *See page 233.*

Velvet shank

Flammulina velutipes

Sticky orange cap, velvety stem, pale gills, tufted

Cap convex, but soon
flattened with a raised
centre, orange yellow,
sticky to slimy, smooth

Gills adnexed, white,
broad, moderately spaced

Spore print

Stem tough, tapering at the
base, yellowish above, becoming
blackish brown below, covered
with a dark brown velvety layer

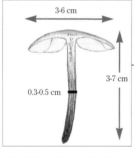

3-6 cm

3-7 cm

0.3-0.5 cm

Flesh fairly thin, soft, white

Frequency common

Spore deposit white

A tufted mushroom which grows on deciduous trees during the winter months. It is available for eating both from the wild and in its cultivated state. Cultivation developed in the Far East, especially in Japan, where it is given the commercial name of 'Enoki-take'. These cultivated forms have a cap which is scarcely formed, whilst the stem is well developed but very pale. Although not one of the tastiest of the edible species it is popular as it is resistant to frost and grows in winter.

EATING

In order to prepare the wild mushrooms for consumption, the sticky pellicle of the cap must first be peeled away. The fruitbodies are generally used for soups.

Habitat
Tufted on deciduous trees, especially elm

LOOKALIKES

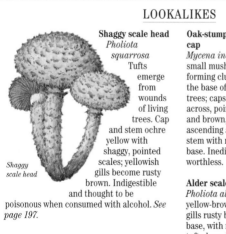

Shaggy scale head

Shaggy scale head
Pholiota squarrosa
Tufts emerge from wounds of living trees. Cap and stem ochre yellow with shaggy, pointed scales; yellowish gills become rusty brown. Indigestible and thought to be poisonous when consumed with alcohol. *See page 197.*

Oak-stump bonnet cap
Mycena inclinata A small mushroom forming clumps at the base of oak trees; caps 2-3 cm across, pointed and brown, gills ascending and white, stem with reddish brown base. Inedible and worthless.

Alder scale head
Pholiota alnicola Bright yellow-brown sticky cap, gills rusty brown, stem pale yellow, russet at base, with ring-zone, strong aromatic smell, tufted on alder. Worthless.

Oak-stump bonnet cap

Southern poplar mushroom

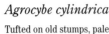

Agrocybe cylindrica

Tufted on old stumps, pale cap and stem, clay-brown gills, large ring on stem

Cap convex, pale brown becoming creamy to ivory yellow, smooth and silky, somewhat wrinkled and sometimes cracked at the centre

Gills at first pale, becoming brown, slightly decurrent or with a decurrent tooth, broad, crowded

Stem cylindrical, white, staining rusty brown towards the base, bearing a persistent, membranous, large, white ring

Spore print

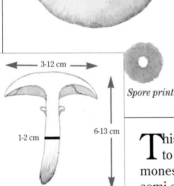

3-12 cm

1-2 cm · 6-13 cm

Flesh mostly white, brown under the cap cuticle and in the stem base; at first smells slightly mealy, becoming rancid, reminiscent of old wine-casks

Frequency locally common

Spore deposit brown

This is a robust, tufted species, unlikely to be confused with any other. It is commonest in southern Europe, where it is semi-cultivated, and much scarcer in the north. It was a popular edible mushroom with the Ancient Romans.

It can be recognized by the pale cap, the ring on the stem, and by the fact that it grows in dense clusters.

The species is also known by the alternative names of *Pholiota cylindracea* and *Agrocybe aegerita*.

EATING

Excellent, with a nutty taste.

48

Habitat
Grows in clusters on old stumps and trunks, especially of poplar, willow and elm

LOOKALIKES

Spring mushroom
Agrocybe praecox More common but appearing in the springtime, on the ground amongst grass; cap 3-7 cm across, cream colour, stem whitish with hanging ring, and a strong smell of meal; edible but not recommended. The hard field cap, *Agrocybe dura*, is more robust; the pale cap surface usually cracks.

The gypsy

Rozites caperatus

Pale powdery cap, brown gills, pale stem with hanging ring

Cap at first strongly rounded with grey-violaceous tints, then expanding, with a central hump and an upturned, wavy margin, dull straw yellow to orange-brown, dry and silky, with a hoary-powdery covering from the universal veil

Spore print

Gills adnate, off-white becoming clay brown; broad, often vertically wrinkled, crowded

Stem cylindrical, pale greyish to yellowish ochre, often streaky, with a prominent, white, membranous ring attached towards middle

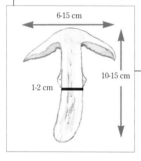

6-15 cm

10-15 cm

1-2 cm

Flesh thick, firm, white, with a faint but pleasant smell but bitter taste

Frequency common in central and northern Europe, but extremely rare in Britain except for Scotland

Spore deposit rusty brown

Often occurring in large numbers on the acidic, sandy soil of the forest, this species prefers northerly or mountainous localities within Europe. In Finland, it is known as 'granny's nightcap'. The gypsy is closely related to the web caps (*Cortinarius* species), most of which must be avoided, but is easily distinguished by the conspicuous, membranous ring on the stem. This ring may cause confusion with the true mushrooms (*Agaricus*) but the brown gills and spore deposit are distinctive.

EATING

Highly prized in central Europe and southern Scandinavia. A good edible species. Must be cooked to remove the bitter taste.

Habitat
On acidic, sandy soil, under coniferous trees in northern Europe, and beech trees in central Europe

LOOKALIKES

Thin-capped web cap
Cortinarius anomalus Has a similar 'frosted' appearance but cap surface is a darker brown; stem has lilac tints towards the top, and lacks a membranous ring but does have a ring-zone of brown fibrils; poisonous.

Wine cap
Stropharia rugosannulata Massive mushroom, weighing up to 4.25 kg, also known as 'burgundy mushroom' and 'Gartenreise'; occurs in eastern Europe but very rare in Britain. Cap up to 25 cm across, purplish brown, sticky, purplish brown gills, thick stem with purplish ring. Cultivated on straw.

Buff meadow cap

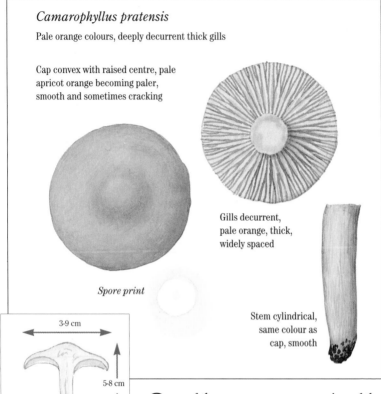

Camarophyllus pratensis

Pale orange colours, deeply decurrent thick gills

Cap convex with raised centre, pale apricot orange becoming paler, smooth and sometimes cracking

Gills decurrent, pale orange, thick, widely spaced

Spore print

Stem cylindrical, same colour as cap, smooth

3-9 cm

5-8 cm

1-1.5 cm

Flesh thick, creamy white, with faint smell

Frequency very common, especially in northern Europe

Spore deposit white

One of the more common species of the wax cap family, the buff meadow cap is sometimes called the meadow wax cap, or the butter mushroom. It may be found in meadows and on lawns, often with other species of wax cap, and can be confused with the chanterelle (page 24). It sometimes forms fairy rings.

Wax caps are named for their wax-like, thick gills, and are easy to recognize by the fine connecting ridges that link the bases of the gills.

EATING

Excellent. A firm flesh rarely attacked by insect larvae, requiring slow cooking as with the wood urchin (see page 30).

Habitat
In grasslands,
sometimes open
woodland

LOOKALIKES

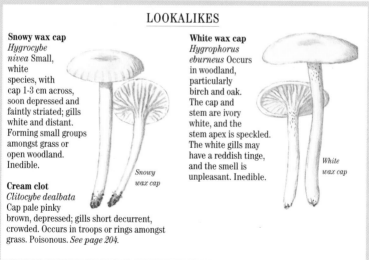

Snowy wax cap
*Hygrocybe
nivea* Small,
white
species, with
cap 1-3 cm across,
soon depressed and
faintly striated; gills
white and distant.
Forming small groups
amongst grass or
open woodland.
Inedible.

*Snowy
wax cap*

Cream clot
Clitocybe dealbata
Cap pale pinky
brown, depressed; gills short decurrent,
crowded. Occurs in troops or rings amongst
grass. Poisonous. *See page 204.*

White wax cap
*Hygrophorus
eburneus* Occurs
in woodland,
particularly
birch and oak.
The cap and
stem are ivory
white, and the
stem apex is speckled.
The white gills may
have a reddish tinge,
and the smell is
unpleasant. Inedible.

*White
wax cap*

The miller

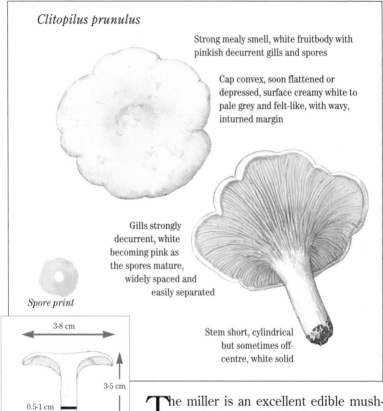

Clitopilus prunulus

Strong mealy smell, white fruitbody with pinkish decurrent gills and spores

Cap convex, soon flattened or depressed, surface creamy white to pale grey and felt-like, with wavy, inturned margin

Gills strongly decurrent, white becoming pink as the spores mature, widely spaced and easily separated

Spore print

Stem short, cylindrical but sometimes off-centre, white solid

3-8 cm

3-5 cm

0.5-1 cm

Flesh soft and rather brittle, white; with a very strong smell and taste of meal or compressed yeast

Frequency common

Spore deposit salmon pink

The miller is an excellent edible mushroom but you should take care not to confuse it with the white funnel caps (*Clitocybe* species). This is one of the pink-spored species and a spore print should be taken to confirm the identity, although the very strong smell is distinctive and may often be detected some distance away. It is sometimes called the plum agaric and the sweetbread mushroom. The surface of the cap feels soft, like a kid glove. Unfortunately, usually found only in small groups.

EATING

Delicious. Cook slowly. Has been used as a substitute for out-of-season oysters.

Habitat
Amongst grass
or open beech
woods; prefers
rich soils,
sometimes in
fairy rings

LOOKALIKES

*Livid pink
gill*

Livid pink gill
*Entoloma
sinuatum* Also
known as
Entoloma lividum.
An uncommon
species, occurring at
edge of woodland. Cap 7-10 cm across,
yellowish brown to greyish, with a short,
greyish stem, and pink, sinuate gills. Very
poisonous. *See page 220.*

Cream clot

Cream clot
Clitocybe dealbata Pinky
brown cap, with white, short
decurrent, crowded gills.
Occurs in troops or rings
amongst grass. Poisonous.
See page 204.

Common white fibre cap
Inocybe geophylla A common species
appearing in troops in woodland. Fruitbody
pure white, but the gills are adnate and
brown. Poisonous. *See page 200.*

Blue-green funnel cap

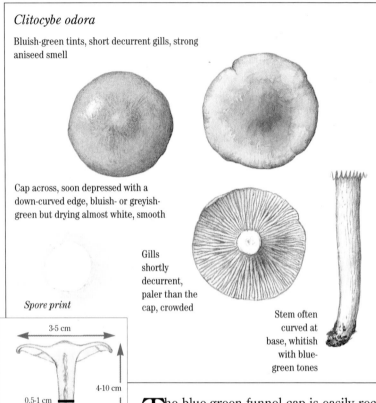

Clitocybe odora

Bluish-green tints, short decurrent gills, strong aniseed smell

Cap across, soon depressed with a down-curved edge, bluish- or greyish-green but drying almost white, smooth

Spore print

Gills shortly decurrent, paler than the cap, crowded

Stem often curved at base, whitish with blue-green tones

3-5 cm

0.5-1 cm

4-10 cm

Flesh thin, white, with a very strong smell of aniseed

Frequency occasional

Spore deposit white

The blue-green funnel cap is easily recognized, sometimes even from a distance, by its strong aniseed smell, a characteristic which gives rise to its alternative name, the aniseed toadstool. There is a white variety which has a similar odour.

Other funnel caps also exist with a similar smell, but they are not edible. Accurate identification is therefore essential.

People do eat it, but the aniseed flavour is rather overwhelming; however, it improves with drying.

EATING

Can be eaten, but more usually dried and used as a spice for flavouring.

Habitat
Amongst humus in leafy woodland, especially under oak trees

LOOKALIKES

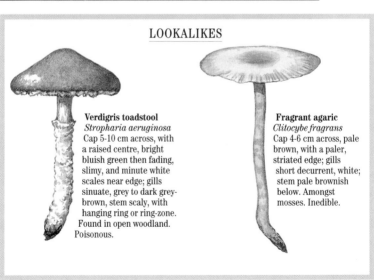

Verdigris toadstool
Stropharia aeruginosa
Cap 5-10 cm across, with a raised centre, bright bluish green then fading, slimy, and minute white scales near edge; gills sinuate, grey to dark grey-brown, stem scaly, with hanging ring or ring-zone. Found in open woodland. Poisonous.

Fragrant agaric
Clitocybe fragrans
Cap 4-6 cm across, pale brown, with a paler, striated edge; gills short decurrent, white; stem pale brownish below. Amongst mosses. Inedible.

The deceiver

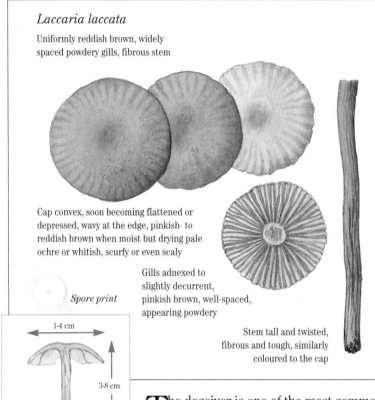

Laccaria laccata

Uniformly reddish brown, widely spaced powdery gills, fibrous stem

Cap convex, soon becoming flattened or depressed, wavy at the edge, pinkish- to reddish brown when moist but drying pale ochre or whitish, scurfy or even scaly

Spore print

Gills adnexed to slightly decurrent, pinkish brown, well-spaced, appearing powdery

Stem tall and twisted, fibrous and tough, similarly coloured to the cap

1-4 cm

3-8 cm

0.4-0.6 cm

Flesh thin, pale reddish brown, watery, odourless

Frequency extremely common

Spore deposit white

The deceiver is one of the most common species throughout Europe but is very variable and there are several closely related species. The name refers to the many forms, which often make identification difficult; added to this, it can look very different in dry and wet weather. However, once you learn to recognize this species it is easily identified by its pinkish-brown fruitbodies with widely spaced, 'powdery' gills. There are always many fruitbodies to be found. The amethyst deceiver invariably grows nearby.

EATING

Best used in stews or mixed with other species because it has little taste. Discard the tough stems.

Habitat
In scattered
troops, amongst
leaf litter in
woods

LOOKALIKES

Russet shank
Collybia dryophila
A small mushroom
with flattened, smooth
cap, and crowded, white gills
contrasting with a smooth,
yellowish-brown stem. Cap 2-5
cm across, flattened, pale
yellow to reddish brown,
drying paler. Amongst leaf
litter in woodlands, especially
with oak, often very
numerous. Worthless and
should never be eaten raw. *Russet shank*

Amongst leaf litter in
leafy woods, especially
under beech.
Poisonous. *See page 208.*

Amethyst deceiver
Laccaria amethystina As
common as the deceiver,
differing only in the uniform
deep violet colour of all parts.
Grows in troops in woodland.
Similarly edible but poor.

Amethyst deceiver

Lilac bonnet cap
Mycena pura One of the larger bonnet caps
species, distinguished by the pink to lilac
colour, and a smell reminiscent of radishes.
Could be confused with amethyst Mycena.

Lilac fibre cap
Inocybe geophylla var. *lilacina* Uniformly
lilac except for the gills which become
brown, and a brown spore deposit. Usually
seen in troops on forest floor. Poisonous.
See page 201.

Two-toned scale head

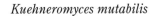

Kuehneromyces mutabilis

A clustered toadstool recognized by the brown, two-tone cap and dark brown, scaly stem with a small ring

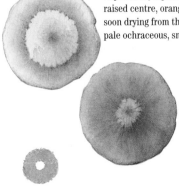

Cap convex, expanding but often retaining a raised centre, orange-brown or date brown, soon drying from the centre which becomes pale ochraceous, smooth

Gills pale to rusty brown, slightly decurrent, crowded

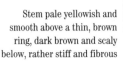

Spore print

Stem pale yellowish and smooth above a thin, brown ring, dark brown and scaly below, rather stiff and fibrous

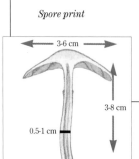

3-6 cm

3-8 cm

0.5-1 cm

Flesh whitish or pale yellowish, with a mild yet pleasant smell and taste

Frequency common everywhere

Spore deposit deep ochre brown

Large clusters of two-toned scale heads with up to a hundred fruitbodies may be found on old stumps and dead tree bases throughout summer and autumn. Rusty brown gills distinguish these from other clustered species; the caps easily absorb water and become paler as they dry out. This fungus is grown commercially in some countries in Europe, and inoculated wood blocks are sold for cultivation at home. It belongs to the same family as the much-cultivated nameko mushroom (*Phaliota* nameko) of Japan.

EATING

Edible and good, but take care to avoid confusion with the marginate pixy cap. Only the caps are eaten as the stems are too fibrous.

60

Habitat
Occurring in clusters on stumps and trunks of deciduous trees

LOOKALIKES

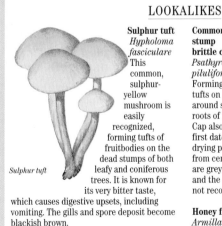

Sulphur tuft

Sulphur tuft
Hypholoma fasciculare
This common, sulphur-yellow mushroom is easily recognized, forming tufts of fruitbodies on the dead stumps of both leafy and coniferous trees. It is known for its very bitter taste, which causes digestive upsets, including vomiting. The gills and spore deposit become blackish brown.

Common stump brittle cap
Psathyrella piluliformis
Forming dense tufts on and around stumps and roots of leafy trees. Cap also two-tone, at first date brown then drying pale clay brown from centre. The gills are grey to dark brown and the stem is white and smooth. Worthless, not recommended for eating.

Common stump brittle cap

Honey fungus
Armillaria mellea Clustered on roots and stumps in late autumn. *See page 44.*

Fawn shield cap

Pluteus cervinus

On rotting stumps; brown, fibrous cap; crowded free
pink gills

Cap convex then flattened, grey to
brown or blackish brown, with small,
fine radial fibres, sticky when moist

Gills free, greyish white
becoming salmon
pink, thin, broad and
very crowded

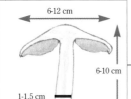

Spore print

Stem cylindrical, solid,
greyish white with darker
small, fine fibres

6-12 cm

6-10 cm

1-1.5 cm

Flesh soft thick, whitish; smell
reminiscent of potatoes or
radish

Frequency common
everywhere

Spore deposit salmon pink

The fawn shield is common on rotting
wood and large specimens, with caps up
to 25 cm across, may be found on sawdust
heaps. Also known by the name *Pluteus atr-
icapillus*, this mushroom is easily identified
and has a long fruiting season. As with all
shield caps, the stem can be readily separated from the cap. This particular one is
variable in stature and colour. Be sure to
collect young, fresh specimens, as they
soon become infested with insect larvae.
The epithet refers to the fawn colour.

EATING

Slightly sharp taste and not to everybody's liking. When
you try the fawn shield cap for the first time, cook it separately and taste a single mouthful. Large, early season
specimens have the strongest flavour.

Habitat
On stumps and
rotting wood

LOOKALIKES

**Willow
shield cap**
*Pluteus
salicinus* Most frequent
on dead willow stumps.
Cap greyish green to
dark green at a slightly
scaly centre; stem white,
slightly green at base,
lacking a smell. Thought
to be poisonous.

**Broad-gilled
agaric**
*Megacollybia
platyphylla* Commonly
found growing on stumps
and buried roots. Cap
greyish brown or paler,
streaky, translucent when
moist; gills whitish, often
splitting; stem white with
conspicuous white cords
at the base. Young caps
are said to be edible but
are not recommended.

Parasol mushrooms

Seeing a troop of parasol mushrooms in open pastureland for the first time is a memorable experience. These include some of the largest of all the mushrooms and, to many, some of the tastiest. In Italy, the **parasol** (*Macrolepiota procera,* page 66) is considered as good as the **Caesar's mushroom** (*Amanita caesarea,* page 98). A few, large caps are sufficient for a substantial meal, and the tough, fibrous stems may be discarded. Although once seen,

Parasol

they are readily recognisable on the next occasion, they have often been confused with at least three other groups of poisonous mushrooms. These are: the smaller, brown *Lepiota* species (see page 174), which also have a scaly cap, free, white gills, and a ring on the stem that can contain dangerous cell-destroying toxins; secondly, the **death cap** (*Amanita phalloides,* page 166) group of species also have the same characteristics and great care must be taken to look for the cup-like volva at the base of the stem; and finally, a widespread species from the warmer regions of the world, the poisonous **green-spored Lepiota** (*Chlorophyllum molybdites,* page 69) very closely resembles the parasols and has appeared on several occasions in Britain and Europe in recent years.

The parasol mushrooms grow in open pastureland and meadows, on roadside embankments, in open woodland and on disturbed soils, such as compost heaps. Many form fairy rings and occur in large numbers. They tend to reappear in the same place, year after year.

Parasols are so-called because they are large and have a parasol or umbrella-like shape with an expanding cap and a tall, straight stem. They are distinguished by their large size and generally tall stature; they have white or pale gills producing a white spore deposit, and a scaly, plate-like cap. The gills are crowded and free from the stem, and there is a large, fleshy ring which becomes loosened and can be moved up and down the stem. The caps can easily be separated from the top of the stem, just like a ball-and-socket joint. It is typical of the parasol mushroom that the tall stem develops and elongates before the cap opens and expands. When fully expanded, the caps are plate-like and may exceed 35 cm across.

The best-known species is the **parasol** (page 66). There are about a dozen species of parasol, some uncommon, others frequent. These include the **flaky parasol** (*Macrolepiota excoriata,* page 69), with a pale brown cap, up to 10 cm across, which breaks into large scales near the margin; the **slender parasol** (*Macrolepiota gracilenta,* page 67), with numerous small brown scales on the cap, up to 12 cm across, and a more or less smooth stem; and the **bossed parasol** (*Macrolepiota mastoidea*) with a pronounced hump at the cap centre, and fine, ochre brown scales.

Equally common, but more often found on disturbed soil and under hedgerows is the **shaggy parasol** (*Macrolepiota rhacodes,* page 68). Although generally regarded as edible, there are a number of recorded cases of gastric upsets, so care needs to be taken when eating them for the first time. In recent times, a species in France, *Macrolepiota venenata*, in many ways similar to the shaggy parasol but with a star-shaped central disk on the cap has caused several cases of severe indigestion.

Shaggy parasol

Parasol mushroom

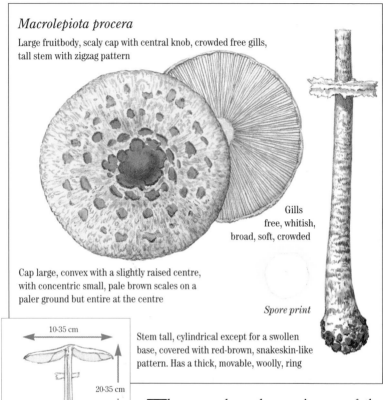

Macrolepiota procera

Large fruitbody, scaly cap with central knob, crowded free gills, tall stem with zigzag pattern

Gills free, whitish, broad, soft, crowded

Cap large, convex with a slightly raised centre, with concentric small, pale brown scales on a paler ground but entire at the centre

Spore print

Stem tall, cylindrical except for a swollen base, covered with red-brown, snakeskin-like pattern. Has a thick, movable, woolly, ring

10-35 cm

20-35 cm

1-2 cm

Flesh firm, whitish, not reddening; with a pleasant smell

Frequency generally uncommon but may be locally common

Spore deposit white

The parasol mushroom is one of the largest and the best of the European edible mushrooms. The taste and texture have been compared to chicken and to oysters. It is often confused with the shaggy parasol but the tall, scaly stem and the non-reddening flesh will readily separate the parasol. Young fruitbodies resemble drumsticks with the fully formed stem bearing a knob-like, unopened cap. Avoid confusion with the much smaller *Lepiota* species (page 174), which have a delicate ring on the stem.

EATING

Excellent strong flavour, and a firm, dry texture; discard tough, fibrous stems. Suitable for slicing and preserving, either by pickling or freezing.

Habitat
Amongst grass in pastures, open woodland and roadside verges, sometimes in fairy rings

LOOKALIKES

Slender parasol
Macrolepiota gracilenta Cap 8-10 cm across, whitish with a distinct raised centre, densely but finely scaly; stem slender, with a fine, banded pattern; edible.

Slender parasol

Stinking parasol
Lepiota cristata Much smaller than most *Macrolepiota* species. Cap has dark, orange-brown scales on white ground. No movable ring on the stem. Also has a distinctive and unpleasant smell. In troops in woods, often at path edges. Possibly poisonous, avoid all *Lepiota* species.

Shaggy parasol
Macrolepiota rhacodes Usually on disturbed soil, gardens, compost heaps, and under shrubs. Cap breaking up into large, coarse scales; stem smooth, off-white discolouring brownish; flesh white discolouring pinkish to orange-red when broken, especially in the stem. Edible but may cause gastric upsets in some people. *See page 68.*

Shaggy parasol

Shaggy parasol

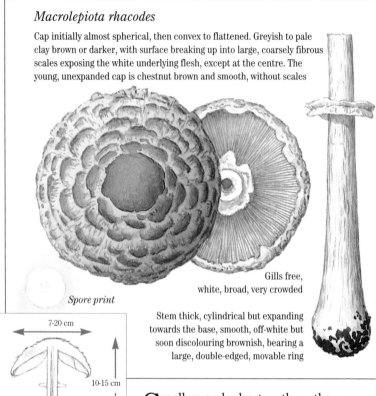

Macrolepiota rhacodes

Cap initially almost spherical, then convex to flattened. Greyish to pale clay brown or darker, with surface breaking up into large, coarsely fibrous scales exposing the white underlying flesh, except at the centre. The young, unexpanded cap is chestnut brown and smooth, without scales

Gills free, white, broad, very crowded

Spore print

7-20 cm

10-15 cm

1-2.5 cm

Stem thick, cylindrical but expanding towards the base, smooth, off-white but soon discolouring brownish, bearing a large, double-edged, movable ring

Flesh thick, white discolouring pinkish to orange-red when broken, especially in the stem; with pleasant smell

Frequency fairly common in gardens

Spore deposit white

Smaller and shorter than the parasol (page 66), the shaggy parasol is a fleshy mushroom with a coarsely scaly cap, white gills and spore deposit, and a stem and flesh that bruise reddish. The ring on the stem is large, double-edged and movable, unlike those of the *Amanita* species. This mushroom is usually found on disturbed or cultivated soil, either solitary, in groups or forming fairy rings.

The variety *bohemica* is more stocky and appears on compost heaps.

EATING

Cap has firm flesh, but discard tough stems. Generally thought edible and tasty but causes digestive upsets in some people, so take care when eating it for the first time.

Habitat
In small groups, usually on disturbed and cultivated soil, at edge of woods or in gardens; often found under shrubbery, on compost heaps or by roadsides. Sometimes amongst needle-litter in conifer woods

LOOKALIKES

Flaky parasol
Macrolepiota excoriata Cap 8-10 cm across, cream, finely downy, with scales towards the edge; stem smooth; ring simple. In meadows, on poor, sandy soil.

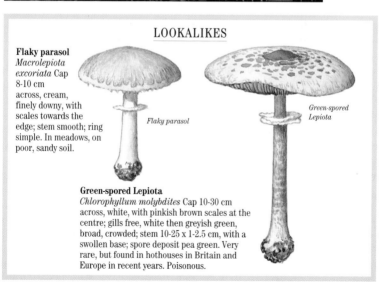

Flaky parasol

Green-spored Lepiota

Green-spored Lepiota
Chlorophyllum molybdites Cap 10-30 cm across, white, with pinkish brown scales at the centre; gills free, white then greyish green, broad, crowded; stem 10-25 x 1-2.5 cm, with a swollen base; spore deposit pea green. Very rare, but found in hothouses in Britain and Europe in recent years. Poisonous.

Fairy ring mushrooms

There are about sixty mushroom species capable of forming fairy rings. These are mostly seen in grassland but are also found in woodlands. 'Fairy rings', 'fairy courts', 'fairy dances', 'fairy walks' and 'hag tracks' are British terms used over the centuries, although these rings can be found in grasslands all over the world. They form part of the folklore of almost every country and, in Britain, are referred to by many poets and writers, including Chaucer, Shakespeare, Tennyson and Kipling. The association with fairies extends throughout Britain, Denmark, France, Sweden, and even the Philippines, and in children's books the mushrooms are often seen as either fairy tables or seats for the musicians to sit upon as the fairies dance. Other countries have regarded them with greater suspicion, and they are associated with witches in Germany, and referred to as the *ronds de sorcières* (witches' rings) in France. Lightning, moles and ants are still blamed for their appearance, even though their true relationship with fungi was recognized more than 200 years ago.

There are three types of fairy ring:

1 Destructive rings that kill or badly damage the grass, and appear as two dark green rings of stimulated grass, separated by a zone of bare earth, as the underground mushroom mycelium either parasites the grass roots or forms a barrier preventing root penetration. This is the fairy ring champignon type (page 72).

2 Rings that stimulate grass growth without doing any damage, for example, the common earthball (page 116).

3 Mushrooms that grow in rings but have no effect on the grass, such as the wax caps (page 52).

The persistent rings can exist for many years and grow to enormous sizes. Rings have been measured at over 600 metres across and have been estimated to be up to 700 years old, making these fungi amongst the oldest of living organisms. From the air, they have often been mistaken for the remains of ancient settlements.

One of the most familiar of the fairy-ring forming mushrooms is the **fairy ring champignon** (*Marasmius oreades*, page 72); the word 'champignon' is the French for mushrooms generally.

Above *Fairy ring champignon*
Above, right *St George's mushroom*
Right *Cracking funnel cap*

This small mushroom is much despised by ardent gardeners for it appears in early summer and continues through the autumn, forming fairy rings on the lawn which can persist and continue to grow for many years and become very difficult to eradicate. On the other hand, it is an excellent edible species and troops can be admired for their beauty. Although it can be picked in considerable numbers, some care must be taken to avoid picking other species which can grow intermixed with the 'fairy ring champignon' and may look superficially similar but are poisonous. These include the white funnel caps, such as the **cracking funnel cap** (*Clitocybe rivulosa*, page 205) and the **cream clot** (*Clitocybe dealbata*, page 204).

A mushroom which forms some of the largest fairy rings, usually found in fields and, especially on chalky downs is the **St. George's mushroom** (*Calocybe gambosa*, page 74). This is one of the few wild, edible mushrooms available in the spring, and therefore is unlikely to be confused with any other species. However, confusion has occurred in the past with the **poisonous red-staining fibre head** (*Inocybe pyriodora*, page 202).

Fairy ring champignon

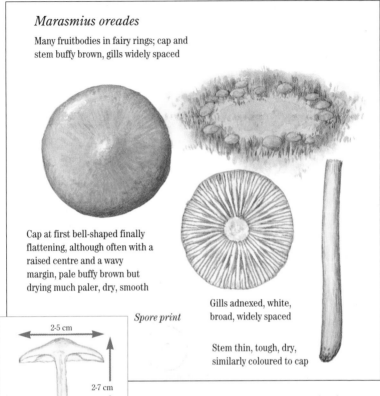

Marasmius oreades

Many fruitbodies in fairy rings; cap and stem buffy brown, gills widely spaced

Cap at first bell-shaped finally flattening, although often with a raised centre and a wavy margin, pale buffy brown but drying much paler, dry, smooth

Spore print

Gills adnexed, white, broad, widely spaced

Stem thin, tough, dry, similarly coloured to cap

2-5 cm

2-7 cm

0.2-0.4 cm

Flesh thin, firm, white, with a smell said to be reminiscent of hay

Frequency very common

Spore deposit white

Fairy ring champignon fruitbodies can appear very suddenly after heavy rain. In Victorian times, it was referred to as 'Scotch bonnet' and sold in marketplaces. In recent years it has reappeared dried in packets in many supermarkets. Although it can be easily collected in enormous numbers, care must be taken to avoid picking the poisonous cream clot which can grow in the same situation and can be intermixed. It is unpopular with gardeners: the fairy rings which it tends to form can be large, and last for many years.

EATING

❌ ❌ ❌

Edible and good, tasting slightly of flour, often used in quantity in stews and casseroles as it has thin flesh. It dries well, and can be kept for years; many claim that the drying process improves the flavour.

Habitat
Growing in large numbers in grassland, especially on lawns where it frequently forms extensive, perennial fairy rings

LOOKALIKES

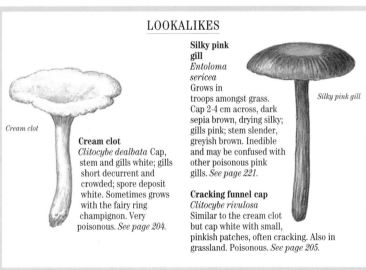

Cream clot

Cream clot
Clitocybe dealbata Cap, stem and gills white; gills short decurrent and crowded; spore deposit white. Sometimes grows with the fairy ring champignon. Very poisonous. *See page 204.*

Silky pink gill
Entoloma sericea
Grows in troops amongst grass. Cap 2-4 cm across, dark sepia brown, drying silky; gills pink; stem slender, greyish brown. Inedible and may be confused with other poisonous pink gills. *See page 221.*

Silky pink gill

Cracking funnel cap
Clitocybe rivulosa
Similar to the cream clot but cap white with small, pinkish patches, often cracking. Also in grassland. Poisonous. *See page 205.*

73

St George's mushroom

Calocybe gambosa

Fleshy pale brown caps with inrolled margin; densely
crowded, whitish gills; strong smell of damp flour

Cap convex, cream to pale brown,
sometimes with grey to reddish
tints, smooth and dry, with a
wavy, inrolled margin

Gills sinuate,
white to cream,
narrow and
densely crowded

Spore print

Stem short and robust,
usually thickened
towards the base, white,
smooth, solid

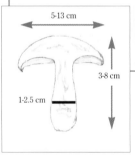

5-13 cm

3-8 cm

1-2.5 cm

Flesh thick, firm, white, with
a strong smell of damp flour

Frequency common

Spore deposit white

This is one of the few wild, edible mushrooms of spring: its English name
derives from its appearance on St George's
Day (21st April). It was well known as an
edible mushroom to the Ancient Romans.
There is a distinctively strong smell and
taste of newly ground flour. In a good season, it is quite easy to collect up to 10 kg at
a time. St George's mushroom is not likely
to be confused with others because so few
fungi appear in spring. Still, beware of the
lookalikes shown opposite.

EATING

Edible but floury smell and flavour makes this a personal
choice. May be eaten fresh or after drying. It is usually
cut into four or five pieces and cooked with any kind of
meat.

Habitat
Large fairy rings
in grassland,
preferring
chalky soils, in
the spring

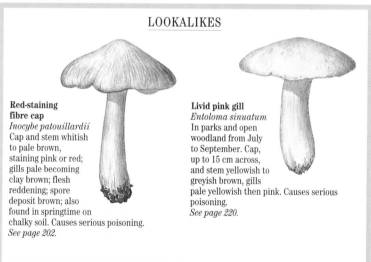

LOOKALIKES

**Red-staining
fibre cap**
Inocybe patouillardii
Cap and stem whitish
to pale brown,
staining pink or red;
gills pale becoming
clay brown; flesh
reddening; spore
deposit brown; also
found in springtime on
chalky soil. Causes serious poisoning.
See page 202.

Livid pink gill
Entoloma sinuatum
In parks and open
woodland from July
to September. Cap,
up to 15 cm across,
and stem yellowish to
greyish brown, gills
pale yellowish then pink. Causes serious
poisoning.
See page 220.

Blewits

Blewits are fleshy mushrooms that have been popular in Europe for many centuries. They are very common in Britain. A century ago, they were sold in Covent Garden Market in London as 'blewits' or 'blue hats', and they are still sold in open markets throughout Europe. Apart from the cultivated mushroom and possibly the common morel, these were the only mushrooms that were sold in English markets until they fell out of favour. In recent years, mushroom farmers have started to cultivate blewits, and once again they are available in supermarkets.

The blewits like disturbed habitats. They form colonies, often fairy rings, on compost heaps, piles of straw, and general woodland litter, sometimes forming a mat of needles in pine forest. The underlying substrate, comprising soil and leaf mould, is bound together by a violet-coloured, cottony mycelium. They readily absorb water and are best not collected in wet weather.

The blewits get their name, as might be expected, from their violet to lilac colouring (at one time, the colouring was used in the dyeing industry). The **field blewit** (*Lepista personata,* page 80) is found in parks, meadows and on the edge of woods; it has a greyish brown cap, which may be tinged with lilac, and the stem is covered with small, fine violaceous to lilac fibres. The **wood blewit** (page 78) is the better known of the two species, uniformly bluish violet, until the old specimens discolour brownish.

Blewits are late-season mushrooms, surviving until the heavier frosts. The colour alone should make these mushrooms recognizable, but confusion can easily occur, either with the smaller and worthless **amethyst deceiver** (*Laccaria amethystina,* page 59) or, more dangerously, with the **violet web cap** species, such as the **purple web cap** (*Cortinarius purpurascens,* page 79), **the imperial** (*Cortinarius violaceus,* page 79) or with the **small lilac fibre head** (*Inocybe geophylla,* page 201). Here is a case where the colour of the spore deposit can be critical: it is very pale pink in the case of the blewits, rusty brown for the web caps and fibre heads.

Opposite *Wood blewits*

Wood blewit

Lepista nuda

All parts purplish lilac; spore deposit pale pinkish

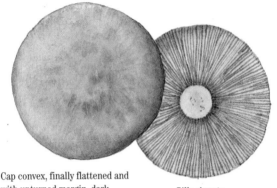

Cap convex, finally flattened and with upturned margin, dark brown to purplish lilac, with a smooth, shiny and dry surface

Gills sinuate, bright violet then discolouring to a dirty flesh-pink, very crowded

Spore print

Stem thick and often with a swollen base, bright violet

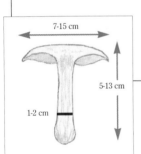

7-15 cm

5-13 cm

1-2 cm

Flesh thick, firm, pale or lilaceous, with a faint fruity smell

Frequency common

Spore deposit very pale pinkish

Wood blewits can be found in large numbers during late autumn and winter, growing amongst leaf litter, in clusters or in rings, and sometimes on compost heaps. Although these are sold commercially, some people have an allergic reaction to them, so take care when eating them for the first time. The field blewit (page 80) is less common, and said to have a superior flavour. Do not confuse these species with the violet, purple and lilac web caps, which have brown gills, initially covered by a veil.

EATING

The flavour of the thick flesh is good and strong and has been compared to veal. Some recommend that the fruitbodies should be boiled before further preparation.

Habitat
Amongst leaf litter, including pine needles, sometimes in fairy rings

LOOKALIKES

The imperial

The imperial
Cortinarius violaceus Similar appearance with purplish cap, gills and stem, but the gills are initially covered by a cobweb-like veil. The gills eventually turn brown, and the spore deposit is brown. Poisonous.

Blue-yellow brittle gill
Russula cyanoxantha Most common brittle gill, with purplish to greyish cap but the gills, flesh, stem and spore deposit white. An early, edible species, occurring from July onwards. *See page 88.*

Blue-yellow brittle gill

Purple web cap
Cortinarius purpurascens Large, violet to lilac fruitbodies appearing in large numbers in late autumn and winter.

Field blewit

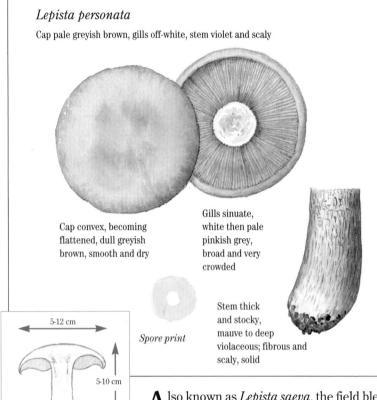

Lepista personata

Cap pale greyish brown, gills off-white, stem violet and scaly

Cap convex, becoming flattened, dull greyish brown, smooth and dry

Gills sinuate, white then pale pinkish grey, broad and very crowded

Spore print

Stem thick and stocky, mauve to deep violaceous; fibrous and scaly, solid

5-12 cm

5-10 cm

1-2 cm

Flesh thick and firm, white, with a floury smell

Frequency occasional to fairly common

Spore deposit pale pinkish

Also known as *Lepista saeva*, the field blewit is a large, fleshy mushroom, similar to the wood blewit (page 78), apart from the lack of any lilac tints on the cap surface. However, colour variations can lead to confusion between the two species.

The field blewit is somewhat less common than the wood blewit, especially in Britain, where, as rich meadows have declined, numbers have decreased. It is thought to have a superior flavour to that of the wood blewit.

EATING

Excellent with mild taste, and can be dried after slicing.

Habitat
In grassland, often at edge of woods

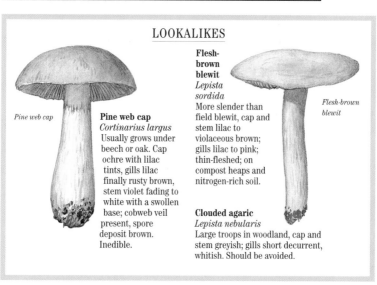

LOOKALIKES

Pine web cap

Pine web cap
Cortinarius largus
Usually grows under beech or oak. Cap ochre with lilac tints, gills lilac finally rusty brown, stem violet fading to white with a swollen base; cobweb veil present, spore deposit brown. Inedible.

Flesh-brown blewit
Lepista sordida
More slender than field blewit, cap and stem lilac to violaceous brown; gills lilac to pink; thin-fleshed; on compost heaps and nitrogen-rich soil.

Flesh-brown blewit

Clouded agaric
Lepista nebularis
Large troops in woodland, cap and stem greyish; gills short decurrent, whitish. Should be avoided.

Brittle gills and milk caps

The brittle gills (*Russula*) and milk caps (*Lactarius*) are amongst the most common and conspicuous mushrooms to be found in European woodlands. There are more than two hundred species known from Britain and Europe, and they are among the most difficult to identify. Many can be classified as edible but few are particularly tasty. Although none contains any toxic material, about half of the species have a hot, peppery taste which can cause stomach upsets, at times severe, and are not to most people's taste. However, in Eastern Europe a number of these hot species are regarded as a delicacy.

The two groups are closely related, belonging to a single family, the *Russulaceae*. The fruitbodies tend to be fairly large and fleshy, and the caps are often brightly coloured – yellow, blues, reds, greens and browns and often combinations of these colours. The flesh is easily broken and has a characteristic crumbly texture (like Cheshire cheese) and the stems are never fibrous. All have a white, cream or yellowish spore deposit. The milk caps differ from the brittle gills in the release of a latex or fluid, often white and milky in appearance, although it may be yellow, red, blue or, rarely, colourless.

The second difference lies in the gill attachment, which appears decurrent in the milk caps, adnexed to adnate in the brittle gills (see page 11). All have a mycorrhizal (interdependent) relationship with the roots of trees, often specific to a particular tree species, so that the species found in conifer woods tend to be quite different from those that occur among leafy trees. Separating the species is difficult, relying on the examination of many microscopical structures.

Saffron milk cap cross section

Once these fungi can be recognized they can often be picked during the autumn months in large quantities. They last for several days, but are prone to insect attack, and care must be taken to pick them only when young and fresh. It is best to parboil any of these species before eating. Always avoid eating them raw. A fragment on the tip of the tongue will alert you to whether or not it is peppery.

The pine-wood milk cap species, the **saffron milk cap**

Apple brittle gill

Below *Bloody milk cap*

(*Lactarius deliciosus,* page 92) and the related **bloody milk cap** (*Lactarius sanguifluus*, page 93) are two of the more popular. Their names relate to the fact that they release an orange or reddish fluid when the fruitbody is broken open. They have a long history as edible mushrooms, mentioned by Pliny the Elder (AD 23–79), and can be found decorating frescoes in Pompeii.

Amongst the edible brittle gills are the **common yellow brittle gill** (*Russula ochroleuca*, page 84), the **cracked green brittle gill** (*Russula virescens*, page 86), and the **apple brittle gill** (*Russula paludosa*, page 90).

Common yellow brittle gill

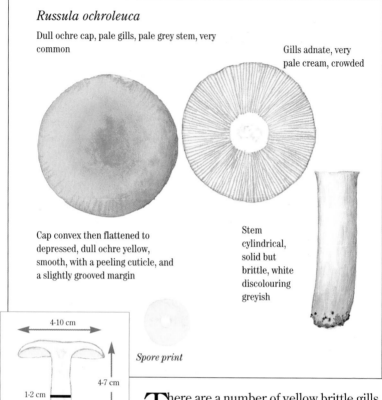

Russula ochroleuca

Dull ochre cap, pale gills, pale grey stem, very common

Gills adnate, very pale cream, crowded

Cap convex then flattened to depressed, dull ochre yellow, smooth, with a peeling cuticle, and a slightly grooved margin

Stem cylindrical, solid but brittle, white discolouring greyish

Spore print

4-10 cm

4-7 cm

1-2 cm

Flesh thick, white, with a mild taste which becomes slowly peppery, no distinctive smell

Frequency very common

Spore deposit pale cream

There are a number of yellow brittle gills, some of which have a distinct and unpleasant peppery taste. Avoid these – the rest have an acceptably mild flavour.

The common yellow is the most common of the yellow brittle gills, and is generally found throughout the autumn months in large numbers.

Although not generally eaten in Britain, it is enjoyed in Scandinavia and Central Europe. The mildly acrid taste can be removed by parboiling.

EATING

✖ ✖ ✖

Taste moderate but not highly recommended.

Habitat
In both coniferous and leafy woodland

LOOKALIKES

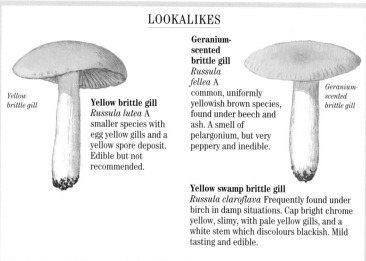

Yellow brittle gill

Yellow brittle gill
Russula lutea A smaller species with egg yellow gills and a yellow spore deposit. Edible but not recommended.

Geranium-scented brittle gill
Russula fellea A common, uniformly yellowish brown species, found under beech and ash. A smell of pelargonium, but very peppery and inedible.

Geranium-scented brittle gill

Yellow swamp brittle gill
Russula claroflava Frequently found under birch in damp situations. Cap bright chrome yellow, slimy, with pale yellow gills, and a white stem which discolours blackish. Mild tasting and edible.

Cracked green brittle gill

Russula virescens
Sea-green mottled cap, creamy gills, stocky white stem

Gills decurrent, creamy white, crowded

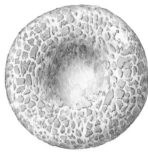

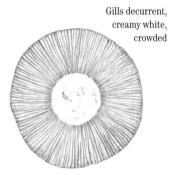

Cap convex soon flattened, often depressed, at first cream becoming sea green with darker patches, the cuticle cracking into small patches to reveal white flesh and appearing mottled; sticky when moist

Stem sturdy, cylindrical, white bruising brown

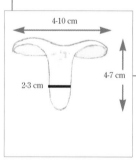

4-10 cm

2-3 cm

4-7 cm

Spore print

Flesh fairly thick, white, with a smell of hazelnuts and a mild taste

Frequency occasional, more common in southern Europe

Spore deposit white

The cracked green brittle gill is generally regarded as the best of the edible brittle gills, but unfortunately it is rather uncommon in Britain.

This is one of several edible green species, but its mottled appearance makes it fairly easy to identify.

It is especially popular in Italy, where it is sometimes eaten raw. The fruitbodies are chopped into small pieces and added to a mixture of olive oil and various seasonings – a tasty dish served cold as a salad.

EATING

The slightly acrid taste disappears on cooking; best fried. Beware of insect-infested fruitbodies.

Habitat
Under beech
and oak

LOOKALIKES

Grass-green brittle gill

Grass-green brittle gill
Russula aeruginea Cap grey-green to yellowish green with a darker smooth centre, not mottled; forking, yellowish gills. Found under birch. An acrid taste makes it inedible.

Shell-fish scented brittle gill
Russula xerampelina Cap colour variable, purplish, brown or straw yellow, or a combination. Recognized by a distinctive smell and taste of crab which affects the dish. Edible.

Shell-fish scented brittle gill

Tooth-gill brittle gill
Russula heterophylla Cap green or yellowish green, smooth, slimy when moist, with very crowded and forking gills, stem whitish. Edible and good with a mild taste.

Death cap
Amanita phalloïdes No green mushroom must ever be confused with the death cap. Look for free gills, a hanging ring on stem and a white cup-like volva at stem base. Deadly. *See page 166.*

Blue-yellow brittle gill

Russula cyanoxantha

Cap purple to grey, gills, stem and spores white; mild taste

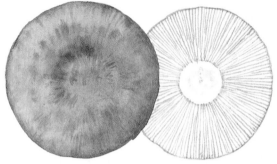

Gills adnexed, white, crowded, with some forking

Cap strongly convex then expanding, firm to hard, usually purplish to greyish but often with green or brownish tints, smooth, greasy when wet

Stem cylindrical, brittle, white, sometimes flushed purplish

Spore print

5-15 cm

5-10 cm

1-3 cm

Flesh thick, white, with little smell and a mild taste

Frequency very common

Spore deposit white

The blue-yellow brittle gill is one of the most common of all the brittle gills, appearing from early July onwards, some years in large numbers. In mainland Europe, the species is often called the parrot russula, owing to its colour variation.

It is, in fact, very variable in colour. Some forms are slate grey, violet or even greenish, making identification difficult for the inexperienced. Its old English name was the 'charcoal burner', referring to the way it used to be cooked.

EATING

Good edible species with firm flesh. Often pickled in mainland Europe.

Habitat
Troops in leafy
woods and
parkland

LOOKALIKES

*Fragile
brittle gill*

Fragile brittle gill
Russula fragilis
Common, delicate and
fragile species, with
cap 2-5 cm across,
purplish or violaceous
but often paler, with a
grooved margin. Stem,
gills and spores white. Smell of apples but
very peppery and inedible.

Blue-green brittle gill
Russula parazurea Similar to blue-yellow
brittle gill, but cap has a powdery bloom.

**Bare-toothed
brittle gill**
Russula vesca Cap
buffy brown, with
green tints, cuticle
contracting at edge
to reveal white gills.
Under beech and
oak. Excellent with
nutty taste and
fruity smell, often
pickled.

*Bare-toothed
brittle gill*

Apple brittle gill

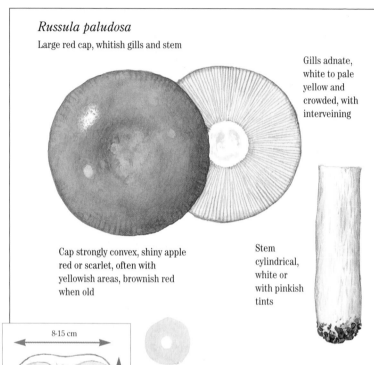

Russula paludosa

Large red cap, whitish gills and stem

Gills adnate, white to pale yellow and crowded, with interveining

Cap strongly convex, shiny apple red or scarlet, often with yellowish areas, brownish red when old

Stem cylindrical, white or with pinkish tints

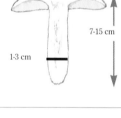

8-15 cm

7-15 cm

1-3 cm

Spore print

Flesh thick, white, with a slightly acrid taste

Frequency rare in Britain, much more common in Scandinavia and northern Europe

Spore deposit deep cream

Most red species have a peppery taste and are not normally eaten, but this large mushroom is an exception: it has a mild taste and is frequently found in marketplaces, especially in Finland, where it is especially popular.

The apple brittle gill is extremely rare in Britain, possibly limited to Scotland, and there confined to the edges of swamps, among peat moss. Young, fresh fruitbodies have a shiny red cap resembling an apple; older ones may be brownish red.

EATING

✗ ✗ ✗

Edible and moderately good.

Habitat
In conifer
woods, near
swamps

LOOKALIKES

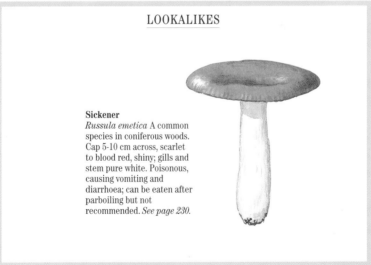

Sickener
Russula emetica A common
species in coniferous woods.
Cap 5-10 cm across, scarlet
to blood red, shiny; gills and
stem pure white. Poisonous,
causing vomiting and
diarrhoea; can be eaten after
parboiling but not
recommended. *See page 230.*

Saffron milk cap

Lactarius deliciosus

Large, reddish orange mushroom, bruising green; abundant orange latex; stem pitted

Cap convex, soon depressed with an incurved margin, reddish orange with several concentric darker zones, slimy when moist, staining green

Gills adnate to short decurrent, pale orange-yellow, staining green, crowded

Spore print

Stem short, orange, often pitted, staining greenish

5-20 cm

3-8 cm

1-1.5 cm

Flesh thick, yellowish cream, with a fruity smell, and releasing copious amounts of orange latex

Frequency very common

Spore deposit pale pinkish cream

Although edible, the saffron milk cap is not considered to be as good as the name suggests: it has a rather granular texture and a resinous taste. It is especially popular in eastern European countries, where it is often pickled. The orange colours can be quite discouraging to the British taste.

The related *Lactarius deterrimus* grows with spruce, has a cap which is uniformly coloured or with faint, narrow, darker zones, and the stem is not pitted, but often has a whitish zone below the gills.

EATING

✗✗✗

Probably best quickly grilled; does not dry well.

Habitat
Often in large numbers under conifers, especially pines

LOOKALIKES

Bloody milk cap
Lactarius sanguifluus
Cap 9-12 cm across, reddish, with pinkish vinaceous zones, powdery, only slightly discolouring green; gills vinaceous pink; stem reddish-purple, with vinaceous pits; the red-vinaceous flesh releases a similarly coloured latex. Under pine, more common in France.

Bloody milk cap

Woolly milk cap
Lactarius torminosus A common species found under birch in wet places. Cap shaggy and woolly, with concentric pinkish zones; exuding a white, very acrid latex, and a smell of pelargonium. Inedible.

Woolly milk cap

Liquorice milk cap
Lactarius helvus Occasional under conifers; cap greyish yellow-brown, with paler yellow gills and a hollow stem The flesh gives out a clear, watery latex and a liquorice smell, especially when dried. Tastes mild, but is poisonous.

93

Orange-brown milk cap

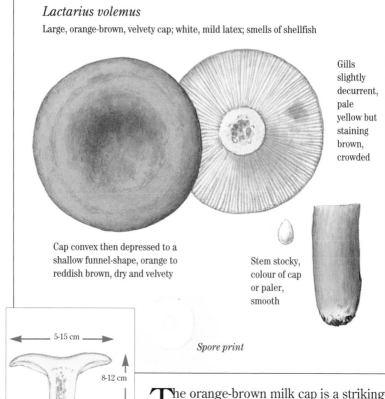

Lactarius volemus

Large, orange-brown, velvety cap; white, mild latex; smells of shellfish

Gills slightly decurrent, pale yellow but staining brown, crowded

Cap convex then depressed to a shallow funnel-shape, orange to reddish brown, dry and velvety

Stem stocky, colour of cap or paler, smooth

Spore print

5-15 cm

8-12 cm

2-3 cm

Flesh firm, yellow with brownish patches, releasing a copious, white, mild latex, and with a smell of boiled shellfish

Frequency uncommon

Spore deposit white

The orange-brown milk cap is a striking-looking, large mushroom, always easy to recognize.

Although always uncommon, it is eaten throughout Europe as it has a delicious, almond-like taste when well cooked. It is often served fried and may also be preserved in salt. In Germany, it is sometimes eaten raw, with salt.

The overall appearance gives the name *volemus*, which is derived from *Volema pira*, a species of large pear.

EATING

Tastes of almonds, and is excellent when thoroughly cooked.

Habitat
Usually under oak

LOOKALIKES

Ugly milk cap
Lactarius necator Also known as *Lactarius turpis*, and *Lactarius plumbeus*. Often difficult to see in long grass, under birch. Cap up to 20 cm across, greenish brown to almost black, sticky, with orange, inrolled margin; gills yellowish and very crowded; stem short and stocky. Gives out a peppery latex. Edible after parboiling.

Ugly milk cap

Curry-scented milk cap
Lactarius camphoratus Amongst conifers. Cap with small raised centre, reddish brown, dry; gills pale reddish brown; exuding a watery white, mild latex. Strong spicy smell makes it useful, when dried and powdered, as a condiment.

Curry-scented milk cap

Northern milk cap
Lactarius trivialis Cap large, grey lilac to yellowish grey, faintly zoned; paler, swollen stem; with white, acrid latex. Valued in eastern Europe; must be boiled.

Coconut-scented milk cap
Lactarius glyciosmus A strong coconut smell. Cap greyish lilac, with pinkish buff gills, and a white, mild latex. Fairly common under birch. Edible but not recommended.

Amanita species

There is no common English name for species of the genus *Amanita*, even though they include some of the best-known edible and the most deadly of poisonous mushrooms. The key characteristics of *Amanita* mushrooms are:

1 A cap which is easily separated from the stem.
2 Gills which are free from the stem, and white (or, rarely, yellow).
3 A ring on the stem, except for the grisettes.
4 A volva at the stem base, which may be cup-like or reduced to a few scales, and
5 A white spore deposit.

Most of these features result from the developmental stages of the fruitbody. The primordial stage resembles a half-buried egg-like structure, protected by a white membrane called the universal veil. Inside the 'egg', is a swollen stem base, and above, the unopened cap. Under the cap are the developing gills which are, in turn, protected by another membrane called the partial veil. The stem elongates to break the universal scales leaving scales on top of the cap and a cup-like volva at the stem base. Finally the cap expands, rupturing the partial veil to leave a ring on the upper stem.

The name is derived from Amanos, a mountain to the north of Syria which was renowned for an abundance of edible mushrooms; an association between mankind and some of the edible species dates back to Antiquity. The emperors of Ancient Rome feasted on only two mushrooms, the **penny bun bolete** (*Boletus edulis*, page 120) which was known as *porcinus* and

Caesar's mushroom (*Amanita caesarea*, page 98), which was confusingly referred to as 'boletus'.

Dried fruitbodies of the **fly agaric** (*Amanita muscaria*, page 212) were traded extensively

Caesar's mushroom

in north-east Asia for medicinal purposes and as an intoxicant until the arrival of vodka, and also used extensively in Russia and eastern Europe as a decoction with milk to paralyse and kill flies, hence the name. Cooked fruitbodies of the **blusher** and the **grisettes** are extensively eaten in Europe. A number of species have been used in forestry and plantations, as they form mycorrhizal (interdependent) associations with many trees.

Death cap

On the other hand, many *Amanita* are poisonous. Do not attempt to eat any *Amanita* species unless you are absolutely sure of your identification. The **death cap** (*Amanita phalloides*, page 166) is the world's most poisonous mushroom, with the **destroying angel** (*Amanita virosa*, page 169) and the **spring Amanita** (*Amanita verna*, page 170) almost equally dangerous.

Serious poisoning also can be encountered with the **panther** (*Amanita pantherina*, page 214) and the **fly agaric** (*Amanita muscaria*, page 212), the **blusher** (*Amanita rubescens*, pages 102, 182), and the **grisettes** (*Amanita fulva*, page 100 and *Amanita vaginata*, page 184) are poisonous if eaten raw.

Panther

Fly agaric

Whether the species is edible or poisonous, keep it separate from other mushrooms in your basket.

Grisette

Caesar's mushroom

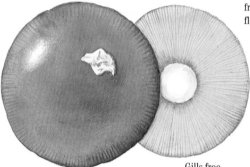

Amanita caesarea

Large mushroom with bright red cap, yellow gills and stem, a hanging ring and a cup-like volva at stem base

Stem egg yellow, smooth, not scaly, bearing a yellow, hanging ring towards the top and growing from a large, white, fleshy, cup-like volva

Cap strongly rounded to convex, finally expanding, brilliant orange-red, smooth and shiny, with a finely striated edge, and occasional white patches of broken veil

Gills free, sulphur yellow to egg yellow, broad and crowded

Spore print

5-20 cm

8-15 cm

1-2 cm

Flesh thick, white, firm, yellow just below the cap surface, with a weak yet pleasant smell

Frequency not uncommon and can be found in great abundance

Spore deposit white

Remarkably, this highly prized, edible mushroom belongs to the same group, the *Amanita* species, as the most toxic of poisonous mushrooms, including the death cap, (page 166). Served in Italian restaurants, and sold in markets in Italy, Spain and southern France. If collecting, take great care not to confuse this with other *Amanita* species. The Emperor Claudius is reputed to have been murdered by his wife, Agrippina, in AD 54, when she provided a dish of this mushroom soaked in juice from the death cap.

EATING	Delicious, with a sweet and nutty taste. All parts edible, especially the cap.
✘ ✘ ✘	

Habitat
Confined to southern Europe, and a Mediterranean climate; especially associated with oak and chestnut, rarely under conifers

LOOKALIKES

Fly agaric
Amanita muscaria
Sometimes called the false orange mushroom in France, it is poisonous, containing ibotenic acid and muscarine, *see page 212*. The cap is a reddish vermilion, with numerous, small, white veil scales, the gills are white and the stem is white with a swollen base which lacks a cup-like volva but has small rings of scales. Widespread throughout Europe under conifers or birch.

Death cap
Amanita phalloïdes
Deadly poisonous, even in small amounts. Note the streaky, olive yellow cap, white gills, the white stem with a zigzag pattern, a ring and a cup-like volva. In leafy woods, often oak, sometimes conifers, during the autumn months throughout Europe. *See page 166.*

Tawny grisette

Amanita fulva

Tall mushroom with an orange-brown cap and grooved margin, white gills, and a stem with a cup-like volva but lacking a ring

Cap strongly bell-shaped when young but opens out to become flattened apart from a small, raised centre at maturity, tawny orange deepening to dark reddish brown at the centre, with a margin which is strongly striated to grooved; initially covered by a white veil

Gills are crowded and free from the stem, white and remaining so

Stem tall, slightly tapering above, hollow and rather fragile, whitish, often bearing a faint zigzag pattern of fine scales; emerging from a large cup-like, white, membranous volva but lacking a ring

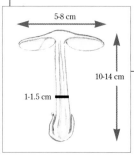

5-8 cm

10-14 cm

1-1.5 cm

Spore print

Flesh thin, white and brittle, with a mild smell

Frequency very common

Spore deposit white

The tawny grisette is commoner in Britain than the grey-capped grisette (page 184), and closely related. It is often eaten in central and eastern Europe, but the quality is moderate, and it is often served with other species. Until recently, only two grisettes were recognized, but now others have been described, forming a largish group. In mainland Europe, the related *Amanita lividopallescens* has a beige to pale brown cap and fragile volva; *Amanita umbrinolutea* has a pale yellow cap with a reddish brown centre.

EATING

Only edible after cooking: the raw form contains poisons that destroy red blood cells. If cooked, must first be parboiled and the water discarded. Only eat if certain of identity.

Habitat
Under leafy trees, where there is lots of leaf litter, often by the sides of paths and on heathland

LOOKALIKES

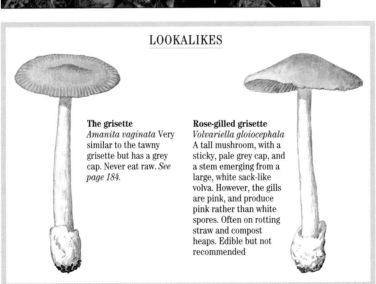

The grisette
Amanita vaginata Very similar to the tawny grisette but has a grey cap. Never eat raw. *See page 184.*

Rose-gilled grisette
Volvariella gloiocephala A tall mushroom, with a sticky, pale grey cap, and a stem emerging from a large, white sack-like volva. However, the gills are pink, and produce pink rather than white spores. Often on rotting straw and compost heaps. Edible but not recommended

101

The blusher

Amanita rubescens

Stocky mushroom, pinkish brown cap with grey scales; reddening flesh and gills; large ring, no volva

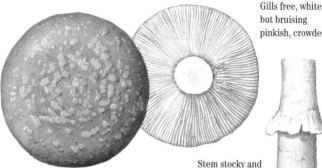

Gills free, white but bruising pinkish, crowded

Cap at first strongly convex and mostly covered with fragmenting grey scales which are easily washed off. They expand to become plate-like. Pinkish to reddish brown, but at times paler or darker

Stem stocky and swollen below, greyish white soon bruising pinkish brown, with a hanging membranous, grooved ring, but the volva reduced to the merest ridge

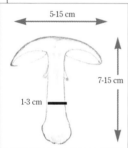

5-15 cm

7-15 cm

1-3 cm

Spore print

Flesh thick, firm, white immediately discolouring red on exposure or around insect holes

Frequency very common

Spore deposit white

Cut open the blusher's flesh and it goes reddish – hence the name. It is an extremely common species, often found in woodlands when little else is available. Avoid confusion with the panther (see opposite). You won't often find a clean specimen – the flesh is popular with mice, snails and insect larvae. This was once a prized edible mushroom in Britain, but is now much less so. It is poisonous if eaten raw – (see page 182). The absence of a volva makes it atypical among the *Amanita* species.

(see page 182)

EATING

Poisonous when raw or poorly cooked, and easily confused with the dangerous panther. If cooked, must first be parboiled and the water discarded.

Habitat
On ground in
small groups in
both leafy and
coniferous
woods

LOOKALIKES

Panther
Amanita pantherina Similar but cap brown and covered with small, white, warty scales; flesh not reddening; volva formed of a ridge and vaguely concentric rings of scales. Mixed woods, prefers beech. Poisonous. *See page 214.*

False death cap
Amanita citrina Very common, with lemon yellow cap, whitish stem with ring and a very swollen base with a rim-like volva; flesh smells of raw potato. Edible but does contain bufotenine, and should be avoided. Easily confused with the death cap.

Ink caps and brittle caps

The ink caps (*Coprinus* species) form a curious group of mushrooms which grow very rapidly and then rot down equally quickly. There are around one hundred of them, most of which can be eaten when young, but they are generally unpleasant or worthless.

Their mode of spore formation and dispersal is highly characteristic. As the spores mature on the gills, the gills rapidly dissolve, or deliquesce, from the edge inwards into a black, ink-like liquid. The colouring is the result of an aggregation of the black spores within the liquid. As the mushroom disintegrates the liquid falls down as drops on to the surrounding substratum, often blades of grass, which are then eaten by animals, such as cows, sheep and rabbits. The heat within the animal's stomach is sufficient to stimulate spore germination after the spores are eliminated by the animal in its dung.

Shaggy ink cap

The black ink has been used in the past for the writing of legal documents. The distinctive, minute spores contained within the liquid can be recognized at a later stage under a microscope, so that any other ink introduced to the document is recognizable. By combining two different species, a unique ink formula can be created. The ink formation is called autodigestion or deliquescence.

Ink caps are generally fragile and thin-fleshed. The caps are often scaly, and the gills are white before blackening. The only one seriously considered to be edible is the **shaggy ink cap** (*Coprinus comatus*, page 106). This is regarded as one of the best of the edible mushrooms and its fruitbodies are probably amongst the most tender. It is very common, sometimes growing in enormous numbers, producing a crop which will cover a large field, at almost any time of year. It will grow in virtually any locality, preferring disturbed soil and areas where there is little competition from other species. As well as growing in the countryside, it is also an urban mushroom, found in parks, by roadsides and buildings, emerging between paving stones and spoiling tennis courts. The **glistening ink cap** (*Coprinus*

Glistening ink caps

micaceus, page 108) is sometimes also eaten. It is a much smaller mushroom which grows in very large numbers on rotten wood.

Common ink cap

Beware of the **common ink cap** (*Coprinus atramentarius,* page 194) which, eaten with alcohol, causes a serious and sometimes persistent poisoning.

Closely related to the ink caps are the brittle caps (*Psathyrella* species), which are similarly fragile, but do not have deliquescent gills. There are many species of these, but very few are regarded as edible, though most are harmless. The only one likely to be eaten is the **common brittle cap** (*Psathyrella candolleana,* page 109).

Shaggy ink cap

Coprinus comatus

Tall cylindrical cap, tiers of white curly scales

Gills free, white becoming grey then black from the edge, and dissolving into a black ink; very densely crowded

Cap tall and cylindrical with a rounded top, only expanding slightly as it matures, pure white except for a pale brown apex, breaking up into tiers of curled, woolly scales, dry, blackening and dissolving upwards from the margin as the gills liquefy, or deliquesce

Stem cylindrical, white, hollow, with a movable ring towards the base

Spore print

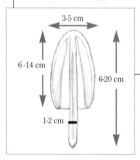

3-5 cm

6-14 cm

6-20 cm

1-2 cm

Flesh thin, white, soft, lacking a distinctive smell

Frequency very common

Spore deposit black

A distinctive mushroom, unlikely to be confused with any poisonous species. It is known as 'shaggy mane' in North America, and as 'lawyer's wig' in Britain because its white cap is covered with tiers of white scales. It is found in fields from spring to late autumn, sometimes in very large numbers. These mushrooms are delicious but need to be picked in early morning, as they soon deteriorate. Choose very young specimens, in which the gills are still totally white, and have not yet started to blacken.

EATING

A strong mushroom flavour; it is usually sliced and fried for breakfast.

Habitat
Commonly found in grassland and parkland, sometimes in very large numbers, and frequently emerging between paving stones in towns

LOOKALIKES

Common ink cap
Coprinus atramentarius Tufted at the base of trees and stumps; cap 5-7 cm across, bell-shaped, with only a few tiny scales at the centre; poisonous when consumed with alcohol. *See page 194.*

Magpie ink cap
Coprinus picaceus
Grows solitary in beech woods, usually on chalky soil. Cap 4-7 cm across, conical and only partly expanding, covered at first by a felt-like, white veil which cracks on expansion to leave large white patches on a dark brown to blackish background. Stem 12-20 cm tall, white and smooth. Not edible.

Glistening ink cap

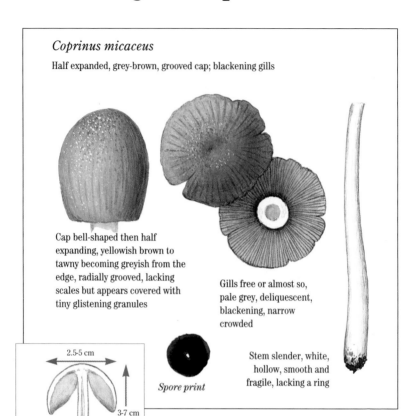

Coprinus micaceus

Half expanded, grey-brown, grooved cap; blackening gills

Cap bell-shaped then half expanding, yellowish brown to tawny becoming greyish from the edge, radially grooved, lacking scales but appears covered with tiny glistening granules

Gills free or almost so, pale grey, deliquescent, blackening, narrow crowded

2.5-5 cm

3-7 cm

0.3-0.5 cm

Spore print

Stem slender, white, hollow, smooth and fragile, lacking a ring

Flesh thin, white, lacking a smell

Frequency very common

Spore deposit black

The glistening ink cap is one of the most common mushrooms to be found in towns, often growing in very large troops and in tufts on dead wood and buried roots. It is known by the common name of 'mica cap' in North America, where it is more popular as an edible mushroom than in Europe.

The mushroom lasts only a few days and should be picked while the gills are still white. Cook immediately, as it will not survive refrigeration.

EATING

Thin-fleshed but the large number of fruitbodies found early in the season make it worthwhile. Collect and cook whilst gills are still white.

Habitat
Densely
clustered on
rotting wood or
buried roots

LOOKALIKES

*Brown
hay cap*

Brown hay cap
Panaeolina foenisecii Very
common from spring
onwards, occurring in short grass,
particularly lawns, hence the
name 'mower's' mushroom. Cap 1-
2 cm across bell-shaped, greyish
brown drying to beige; gills dark
brown, mottled. In groups but not
clustered. Inedible; thought to
contain minute amounts of
psilocin. *See page 191.*

Common brittle cap
Psathyrella candolleana Common from
spring onwards, tufted around stumps. Cap 3-
5 cm across, yellowish cream, with white veil
on edge; gills pink-grey, not deliquescent;
stem white, hollow. Edible.

Weeping widow
*Lacrymaria
velutina* Cap 4-10
cm across, convex
with a raised centre,
yellowish brown, radially
streaked, with a woolly edge;
gills blackish brown, mottled,
with black droplets along the
edge; stem 6-12 x 0.5-1 cm,
whitish, with a fibrous, black
ring zone; tufted in grass,
often by roadsides and
buildings. Although not
generally regarded as
poisonous, this species does
have a bitter taste which can cause gastric
upsets. Recently a near fatality in Scotland
was attributed to the very closely related
Lacrymaria glareosa.

*Weeping
widow*

Puffballs

Common puffballs

The puffballs are amongst the commonest of fungi, and may be found in fields, pastures or woodland, the great majority on the ground. Essentially, the structure is simple, consisting of an outer skin, or peridium, enclosing the spore-producing contents, or gleba. This production of the spores inside the fruitbody instead of on the surface, as in other mushrooms, has traditionally resulted in these fungi being included in an artificial class, the Gasteromycetes, which means 'stomach fungi'. The ripe spores escape either through a hole at the top of the fruitbody, as in the **common puffball** (*Lycoperdon perlatum*, page 114), or by the outer skin flaking away, as in the case of the **giant puffball** (*Calvatia gigantea*, page 112). External pressure, whether from raindrops, air currents or a passing animal, leads to the release of clouds of spores into the air by a puffing action.

Puffballs as edible mushrooms have a long history and widespread use. In Europe, their culinary history dates back to classical times. Care must also be taken not to confuse puffballs with the young, unopened 'egg' stages of the poisonous

Giant puffballs

Amanita species. This can be easily checked by cutting the young fruitbody vertically in half to see if there is any development of gills.

The **giant puffball** (*Calvatia gigantea,* page 112) is probably the easiest of all the fungi to recognize, forming a very large, ball-shaped fruitbody, often 50 cm or more across, and sometimes growing up to 160 cm across. The smooth, soft surface is at first pure white, then gradually discolours to brown as it eventually breaks up and flakes away. The giant puffball is not always common, but in certain years it may be found in large numbers, when it may form fairy rings in open woodland, in grassland or on disturbed soil. Its spore production is prolific. It has been calculated that a large specimen will produce 20,000,000,000,000 spores, which makes it probably the most productive organism on the planet. Of course, only one or two spores will survive and germinate to produce new puffballs, otherwise the progeny would encircle the earth several times over.

The commonest of the puffballs is the **common puffball** (*Lycoperdon perlatum,* page 114), which, like all *Lycoperdon* species has a broad stalk supporting the swollen head. The **stump puffball** (*Lycoperdon pyriforme*, page 115), is unique amongst the puffballs in growing on dead wood rather than on the ground, where it forms large clusters of small, pear-shaped fruitbodies.

Closely related to the true puffballs are the Bovists (*Bovista* species, page 117). These form small, round fruitbodies, lacking the stalk-like base, and frequently become detached from the soil so that they roll around on the ground, pushed by the wind. The spores are released through an irregular tear at the top.

The most specialized and striking of the puffballs are the earthstars (*Geastrum* species), in which the outer layers split open as radiating segments, to reveal an inner spore-sac.

Earthballs (*Scleroderma,* page 117) not to be confused with true puffballs have thick skins and may be eaten in tiny quantities as a condiment, or in truffle dishes. These are not generally considered edible.

Giant puffball

Calvatia gigantea

Large in size, ball-shaped

Fruitbody ball-shaped or nearly so, at first pure white, with a smooth soft surface and a texture of suede, later discolouring yellowish to olive brown with the outer layer gradually flaking away; at first narrowly attached at the base to the soil but becoming free

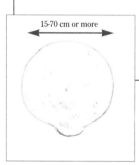

15-70 cm or more

Flesh white and firm but progressively becoming brown and powdery as the spores mature, with a smell of 'mushroom'

Frequency widespread, fairly common

Spore deposit brown

The giant puffball is probably the easiest of all the fungi to recognize. The very large, ball-shaped fruitbody can weigh as much as 20 kg, and 4 kg is frequently recorded. It is not always common, but in some years it can be found in large numbers, when it may form fairy rings in open woodland, in grassland or on disturbed soil such as roadsides or embankments near hedges. Many other smaller puffballs are edible in their young condition, when the flesh is white and firm.

EATING

The flesh is delicious if eaten in the right condition – see above. Cut into slices about 1 cm thick, coat in breadcrumbs, and gently fry in butter for a few minutes.

Habitat
Singly or in groups, sometimes forming large fairy rings, in fields and on road verges

---

LOOKALIKES

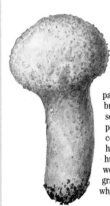

Pestle-shaped puffball
Handkea excipuliformis
Large and pestle-shaped, 5-20 cm tall, pale ochre to grey-brown, finely scurfy; brown powdery gleba confined to upper half. Amongst humus, mostly in woods, sometimes grassland. Edible when young.

Mosaic puffball
Handkea utriformis
Fruitbody up to 15 cm across, almost ball-shaped but with a short and distinct narrower base, with a whitish to grey-brown surface which cracks into more or less polygonal plates; at maturity the upper part breaks open to release the brown spore powder; in grassland. Edible when young.

Common puffball

Lycoperdon perlatum

A common, pear-shaped, white puffball characterized by the surface which bears numerous conical spines, with an opening at the top from which clouds of spores emerge

Sterile base firm, spongy, composed of small cells

Spore print

Fruitbody with a distinct stem-like base, upper part rounded, whitish at first, finally pale brown, with numerous, short, pyramidal spines each surrounded by a ring of smaller warts, leaving a somewhat net-like pattern when rubbed; opening by a small, central hole

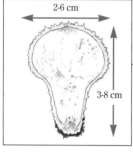

2-6 cm

3-8 cm

Flesh (or gleba) white when young becoming olive brown and powdery as the spores develop.

Frequency very common.

Spore deposit yellowish brown to olive brown

Puffballs are frequently encountered. They appear white and shiny in the early autumn, and the dried remnants persist as brown, powdery containers throughout the rest of the year. The spores escape through a small opening at the top of the puffball when pressure is exerted by raindrops or by passing animal life. There are many puffball species, all of which are edible when the flesh is white. Avoid confusion with unopened toadstools which are initially enveloped by a veil.

Eating

Edible and delicious when young and the flesh is white and moist, but discard once any yellowish brown colour appears.

Habitat
On the ground
amongst leaf
litter, mostly in
open woodland,
plantations, also
in pastures, but
never on wood

LOOKALIKES

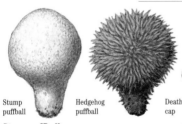

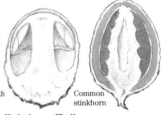

Stump
puffball

Hedgehog
puffball

Death
cap

Common
stinkhorn

Stump puffball
Lycoperdon pyriforme A common species
distinguished by the clustered, pear-shaped
fruitbodies which grow on old stumps and
logs or attached to buried wood, and have
white, cord-like mycelium at the base.
Forming large clusters of smaller fruitbodies,
3-5 cm high, 2-4 cm across above, with a
scurfy surface of tiny warts and granules
becoming smooth.

Hedgehog puffball
Lycoperdon echinatum Locally common but
often rare, mainly in central Europe but
reaching southern Finland and Scotland.
Fruitbodies, found in beech woods, densely
covered with dense dark brown spines, up to
6 mm long, which are easily detached. The
spore deposit is chocolate brown

Meadow puffball

Vascellum pratense

Small, flat-topped puffball; in section, the powdery gleba is separated by a layer

Fruitbody white to ochraceous, with many granular spines (up to 1.5 mm long) which are easily rubbed away; eventually developing an irregular hole at centre

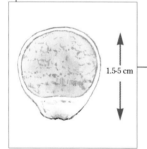

1.5-5 cm

Flesh (or gleba) white and moist becoming grey-brown and powdery

Frequency very common

Spore deposit yellowish brown to olive brown

The meadow puffball is very similar to the common puffball, and is equally good to eat. You may sometimes come across the old fruitbodies, which are brown and parchment-like, having released their spores through the large, torn opening in the top.

This particular puffball is very tolerant to artificial fertilizers, which helps to explain its frequency. It can be found almost anywhere in the world, apart from the tropical lowlands.

EATING

Edible and delicious when young and the flesh is white and moist; but do not eat once any yellowish brown colour appears.

Habitat
In grassland,
including lawns,
prefers drier
localities

LOOKALIKES

Lead-grey Bovist

Lead-grey Bovist
Bovista plumbea Very common and widespread, as small groups amongst short grass, including lawns. Fruitbody 1-5 cm across, ball-shaped, white drying greyish, surface eventually loosening, containing an olive brown gleba, and with a small opening at the top of the puffball. Edible when young.

Brown Bovist
Bovista nigrescens Fruitbody 3-6 cm across, globose, white, becoming free from the substratum; with the surface at first smooth but eventually splitting open at the apex with an irregular tear to release a dark purplish brown spore powder. Mostly on open grassland.

Brown Bovist

Common earthball
Scleroderma citrinum One of several similar earthballs, which have a ball-shaped fruitbody, 4-10 cm across, with a yellowish brown hard outer, scaly layer; lacks a stem. Internally purplish brown, with white veins, and firm in the young stages, becoming brown and powdery. On heaths and in open woodland, especially on sandy soil. Poisonous. *See page 236.*

Boletes

Boletes are mushroom-like fungi, with a soft, fleshy fruit-body consisting of a cap borne on a central stem. Instead of gills on the underside of the cap, however, there are a series of fine, vertical tubes, each opening by a small pore to give a sponge-like appearance. They differ from the tough bracket fungi, or 'polypores', which also have a layer of tubes and pores, in being soft and in rotting within a few days. In addition, the tube-layer of the boletes can be easily removed from the cap. The boletes represent a very large group, with one hundred species or more in Europe, and many more throughout the world. They were formerly placed within a single family, but it is now known that they are not all closely related and at least six families are represented.

They have been renowned for their edible qualities since Classical times, although the 'boletus' of Ancient Rome refers to the unrelated Caesar's mushroom. Fortunately, few species are poisonous. It is advisable to avoid any bolete which has either a red tube-layer on the underside of the cap, or a flesh which discolours bluish violet when exposed. Some species, such as the **bitter bolete** (*Tylopilus felleus*, page 235), have such an unpleasant, bitter taste that it would ruin any meal. As it can be easily confused with the penny bun bolete, collectors should learn to recognize this species.

Most species are large and fleshy and there is a tendency for them to appear early in the fungus season, from late summer onwards. They demonstrate a vast range of colours, particularly reds, yellows and orange and, in many cases, the flesh may change colour quite dramatically when it is broken open and exposed to air.

By far the best known and most popular of the bolete species is the **penny bun bolete**

(*Boletus edulis*, page 120). This is the English name, referring to the brown colour of the cap. Almost every European country has its own name, and in restaurants it will be found under the names of *porcino* from Italy, *Steinpilz* from Germany and, perhaps most commonly, the '*cep*' from France or, under its full title, the '*cèpe de Bordeaux*'. In North America it is referred to as the 'king bolete', and there are several closely related species.

It is so popular in fact that some countries, such as Switzerland, have had to introduce legislation to prevent over-picking.

Closely related to the *Boletus* species are the rough stalks (*Leccinum* species, page 122). These have tall, cylindrical stems bearing numerous, tiny, usually dark, granular scales and, like the *Boletus* species, they are generally closely associated with particular tree species. Most have reddish, brown or orange caps, up to 20 cm wide, and the underlying pore surface is whitish to cream. Altogether there are about twenty species, although some are rare. All are edible but, unfortunately, many are prone to insect attack.

Orange birch rough stalk

Red-capped rough stalk

A much-collected species, and the most striking of the *Suillus* species, is the **slippery Jack** (*Suillus luteus*, page 126) characterized by a slimy cap surface.

Left *Penny bun bolete*
Right *Slippery Jack*

Penny bun bolete

Boletus edulis
Firm and robust; cap yellowish brown, pores whitish;
stem with a white network

Spore print

Cap usually strongly convex, light brown to bronze brown, slightly paler at the margin, smooth, dry or slightly sticky in moist weather, with a rounded margin

Tubes white or cream; pores depressed around the stem apex, whitish to olive-yellow, minute

Stem solid, thickened below, whitish or pale brown, bearing in the upper part a raised network of fine, white lines

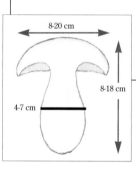

8-20 cm

8-18 cm

4-7 cm

Flesh whitish, not changing colour when cut, thick and hard, with a mild and a pleasant smell

Frequency common

Spore deposit olive brown

Often referred to by the French name, 'cep'. A warm season, with plentiful rain can produce a 'bolete year', when they grow abundantly. There are several closely related species, including the early summer bolete and the later *Boletus pinicola* of coniferous woods. Firm flesh prevents early rotting, but older specimens may contain insect larvae. Popular with squirrels. Fruitbodies are frequently dried for later use in soups, or may be pickled. Look for white net on the stem to avoid confusion with the bitter bolete.

EATING

An excellent edible species, much sought-after. Sold commercially, and also used as a flavouring in soups. Has tender, juicy flesh with a delicate flavour. The spongy tube-layer is normally removed before cooking.

Habitat
On the ground in pine, oak and chestnut woods

LOOKALIKES

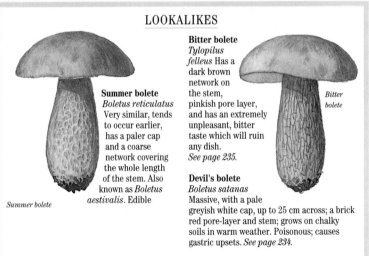

Summer bolete
Boletus reticulatus Very similar, tends to occur earlier, has a paler cap and a coarse network covering the whole length of the stem. Also known as *Boletus aestivalis*. Edible

Summer bolete

Bitter bolete
Tylopilus felleus Has a dark brown network on the stem, pinkish pore layer, and has an extremely unpleasant, bitter taste which will ruin any dish.
See page 235.

Bitter bolete

Devil's bolete
Boletus satanas
Massive, with a pale greyish white cap, up to 25 cm across; a brick red pore-layer and stem; grows on chalky soils in warm weather. Poisonous; causes gastric upsets. *See page 234.*

121

Brown birch rough stalk

Leccinum scabrum
Tall stem with black granules; cap grey-brown, flesh stays white

Cap strongly convex, thick fleshed, greyish brown to yellowish brown, smooth, dry to sticky

 Spore print

Tubes adnexed, deeply sunken around the stem apex, off-white; pores off-white, minute, bruising brownish

Stem tall, off-white, with tiny, black, granular scales

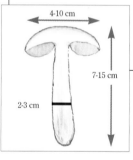

4-10 cm

7-15 cm

2-3 cm

Flesh thick, white, firm, does not discolour when broken open

Frequency very common

Spore deposit cinnamon brown

A very common species, belonging to a group sometimes known as the 'rough stalks' owing to their scaly stems. This is the most common species, together with orange birch rough stalk, which also grows under birch, and the red-capped rough stalk, which grows under aspen. The brown birch rough stalk can be found in large numbers but is subject to insect attack, so look for young, fresh specimens. The related *Leccinum vulpinum* is purplish brown and grows with pine.

EATING

Edible and excellent, after removal of the spongy tube-layer; older stems may have to be peeled.

Habitat
On the ground,
under birches

LOOKALIKES

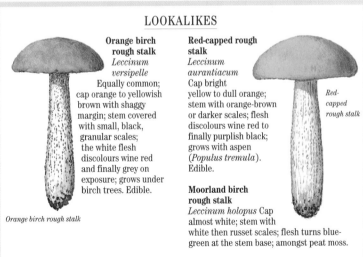

**Orange birch
rough stalk**
*Leccinum
versipelle*
Equally common;
cap orange to yellowish
brown with shaggy
margin; stem covered
with small, black,
granular scales;
the white flesh
discolours wine red
and finally grey on
exposure; grows under
birch trees. Edible.

Orange birch rough stalk

**Red-capped rough
stalk**
*Leccinum
aurantiacum*
Cap bright
yellow to dull orange;
stem with orange-brown
or darker scales; flesh
discolours wine red to
finally purplish black;
grows with aspen
(*Populus tremula*).
Edible.

*Red-
capped
rough stalk*

**Moorland birch
rough stalk**
Leccinum holopus Cap
almost white; stem with
white then russet scales; flesh turns blue-
green at the stem base; amongst peat moss.

123

Orange birch rough stalk

Leccinum versipelle

Reddish orange cap; stem with black, granular scales; flesh blackening on exposure

Tubes adnexed, deeply sunken around the stem apex, yellowish to greyish; pores off-white, minute, bruising brownish

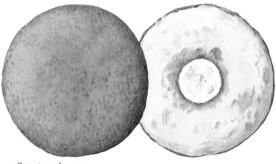

Cap strongly convex, reddish orange to saffron, smooth, dry to slightly sticky when moist, with shaggy edge

Stem tall, off-white, covered over entire length with tiny, black, granular scales

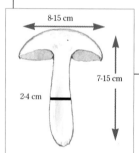
Spore print

8-15 cm

7-15 cm

2-4 cm

Flesh thick, white, firm, discolouring violaceous red and finally blackish when broken open

Frequency very common

Spore deposit cinnamon brown

Also widely known as *Leccinum testaceoscabrum*, the orange birch rough stalk is an excellent edible species. It is frequently found in large numbers wherever birch trees grow, although it also sometimes occurs amongst pine trees and spruce trees in mountainous regions.

The spruce rough stalk (*Leccinum piceinum*) is closely related to the orange birch rough stalk, but has a rusty brown cap and the scales on its stem are at first whitish to brownish.

EATING

Edible and excellent, after removal of the spongy tube-layer; older stems may have to be peeled.

124

Habitat
On the ground, under birches

LOOKALIKES

Poplar rough stalk
Leccinum duriusculum
Cap 8-15 cm across, greyish brown to coffee brown, often finely cracked; tubes greyish bruising pink to brown; stem white, covered with fine, dark brown, woolly scales; flesh bruising pink to pale violaceous. Under poplar. An excellent edible species with a firm to hard flesh.

Poplar rough stalk

Oak rough stalk
Leccinum quercinum Cap up to 20 cm across, brick red to rusty orange, rather scaly; tubes cream to ochraceous buff; stem white, covered with tiny reddish brown to blackish scales; flesh bruising violaceous to blackish. Under oak or beech. Edible.

Oak rough stalk

Yellow-cracking rough stalk
Leccinum crocipodium Cap yellowish brown to cinnamon, velvety, conspicuously cracking; tubes bright yellow; stem yellow, with tiny, yellowish brown scales in lines; pale flesh bruising blackish violaceous. Edible but blackens when cooked.

125

Slippery Jack

Suillus luteus

Cap dark brown, slimy, pores lemon yellow; stem with a large ring

Tubes adnate, pale yellow; pores small, lemon yellow or straw coloured

Spore print

Cap convex, very slimy, dull chestnut brown or chocolate brown with purplish tinge

Stem brownish below, whitish or pale yellowish above, with brownish, glandular dots below the ring; ring large, spreading, membranous, cream or yellowish, darkening as the spores are released from the pore surface

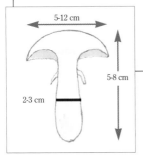

5-12 cm

5-8 cm

2-3 cm

Flesh white, not changing colour when cut; lacking a distinctive smell

Frequency common

Spore deposit clay or olivaceous brown

The slippery Jack is a pine-wood species, particularly common among Scots pine on sandy ground where it can appear in large numbers – although it is often hidden by the fallen pine-needles. The mushroom is characterized by the very slimy, chestnut cap and well-developed ring. As with all the species of *Suillus*, the cap is covered by a slimy surface layer called the pellicle. This layer must be peeled away before cooking the mushroom, as it can cause unpleasant gastric upsets.

EATING

Highly regarded, but best collected in late season when there is little risk of insect attack.

Habitat
Under conifers,
especially pines

LOOKALIKES

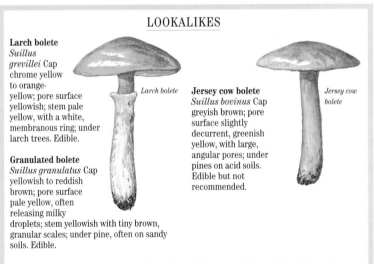

Larch bolete
Suillus grevillei Cap chrome yellow to orange-yellow; pore surface yellowish; stem pale yellow, with a white, membranous ring; under larch trees. Edible.

Larch bolete

Granulated bolete
Suillus granulatus Cap yellowish to reddish brown; pore surface pale yellow, often releasing milky droplets; stem yellowish with tiny brown, granular scales; under pine, often on sandy soils. Edible.

Jersey cow bolete
Suillus bovinus Cap greyish brown; pore surface slightly decurrent, greenish yellow, with large, angular pores; under pines on acid soils. Edible but not recommended.

Jersey cow bolete

Bay bolete

Xerocomus badius
Dark chestnut brown cap; yellowish pores, bluing flesh; slender stem

Spore print

Stem cylindrical or tapering below, paler than cap, fibrous, lacking any net or granules

Cap strongly convex becoming flattened, chestnut brown, sticky when moist, drying finely velvety and shiny

Tubes adnate, dirty yellow, quickly bruising to bluish green when touched

8-15 cm

8-10 cm

1.5-2 cm

Flesh thick and firm, yellowish but turning bluish green on exposure

Frequency common in wet seasons

Spore deposit cinnamon brown

The bay bolete is probably the largest of the *Xerocomus* species, which are characterized by a yellowish pore surface, and a slender stem. Unlike other boletes, such as species of *Boletus*, *Leccinum* and *Suillus*, they don't only grow with the roots of specific trees, and so can be found in large numbers under a range of trees or some distance away, growing on rotting vegetation. This is one of many boletes in which the flesh turns blue on cutting – but not all of these are edible.

EATING

Regarded by some as equal to the penny bun bolete, with a mild taste.

Habitat
On ground in
both leafy and
coniferous
woodland

LOOKALIKES

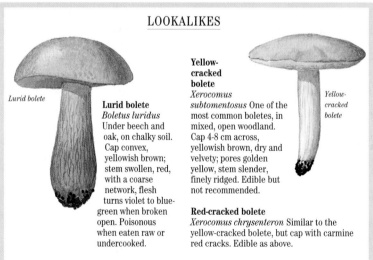

Lurid bolete

Lurid bolete
Boletus luridus
Under beech and
oak, on chalky soil.
Cap convex,
yellowish brown;
stem swollen, red,
with a coarse
network, flesh
turns violet to blue-
green when broken
open. Poisonous
when eaten raw or
undercooked.

**Yellow-
cracked
bolete**
*Xerocomus
subtomentosus* One of the
most common boletes, in
mixed, open woodland.
Cap 4-8 cm across,
yellowish brown, dry and
velvety; pores golden
yellow, stem slender,
finely ridged. Edible but
not recommended.

*Yellow-
cracked
bolete*

Red-cracked bolete
Xerocomus chrysenteron Similar to the
yellow-cracked bolete, but cap with carmine
red cracks. Edible as above.

129

Oyster mushrooms and bracket fungi

This group grows on wood, usually on the side of tree trunks, or from roots, or on dead stumps. Most have a shell- or shelf-like form, hence their names. The oyster mushrooms (*Pleurotus* species) closely resemble other mushrooms in having gills underneath the cap but are often stemless or with only a very reduced stem. They tend to be soft- to firm-fleshy and of only short duration, although they can appear repeatedly throughout the year, being less dependent upon climatic conditions than other mushrooms.

The bracket fungi represent a mixed group, mostly belonging to the polypores, which develop pores on the underside of the cap, in place of gills. They are often tough, growing slowly, so that the fruitbodies can become large and survive for many months, sometimes years.

The **oyster mushrooms** (*Pleurotus* species, pages 132-137) have always been a favourite with mushroom gatherers and are also amongst the easiest mushrooms to cultivate. They are excellent, edible mushrooms, rich in flavour, with a significant protein content, and are attractive on the table. *Pleurotus* species come in a wide range of colours, from white, blue, grey, brown, golden yellow to pink. The **golden oyster** (*Pleurotus citrinopileatus*, page 137) originates from the far east of Russia, but is now frequently encountered in supermarkets, as clusters of beautiful deep yellow caps.

Branched oyster

The closely related **branched oyster mushroom** (*Pleurotus cornucopiae*, page 134) is a whitish mushroom, commonly found on leafy trees throughout Europe. Another striking oyster mushroom of the supermarket is the **pink oyster** (*Pleurotus salmoneostramineus*, page 137), again originating from the far east of Russia. It produces bright pink fruitbodies.

Gastronomically, the best of all the oyster mushrooms is the **king oyster mushroom** (*Pleurotus eryngii*, page 136), naturally only occurring in the Mediterranean region and the steppes of Central Europe. Much research has been done on its cultivation.

Only a very few of the bracket fungi are edible, owing to the toughness of their texture. One exception is the **chicken of the woods** (*Laetiporus sulphureus*, page 140), also known as the sulphur shelf. The young, fresh and moist caps are popularly regarded as a good edible mushroom, but there are confirmed reports that some people are allergic to it, with serious gastric upset and dizziness.

Another edible bracket fungus is the **hen of the woods** (*Grifola frondosa*, page 138), a large, compound polypore, comprising numerous overlapping, greyish brown caps, growing closely together so that it is difficult to see the stems from above. Large specimens can weigh up to 45 kg. This is a popular edible species, especially in Japan, where it is called *maitake* (dancing mushroom).

Cauliflower fungus

The **cauliflower fungus** (*Sparassis crispa*, page 144), also known as the 'brain fungus', is a large fungus resembling the head of a lettuce, rather than a cauliflower, comprising many, ribbon-like, curling branches but with neither gills nor pores on the underside. The fibrous, brittle flesh is best cooked when young, and does not preserve well.

Oyster mushroom

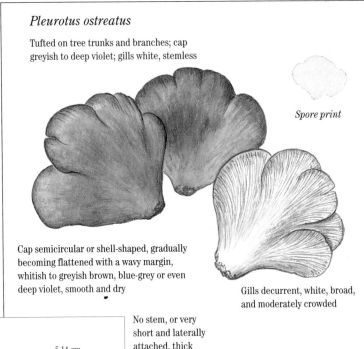

Pleurotus ostreatus

Tufted on tree trunks and branches; cap greyish to deep violet; gills white, stemless

Spore print

Cap semicircular or shell-shaped, gradually becoming flattened with a wavy margin, whitish to greyish brown, blue-grey or even deep violet, smooth and dry

Gills decurrent, white, broad, and moderately crowded

No stem, or very short and laterally attached, thick and solid

5-14 cm

Flesh thick, white, not changing; with a mushroomy or slightly mealy smell

Frequency common

Spore deposit very pale lilac

The oyster mushroom may be found throughout the year, as it is resistant to low temperatures. It grows in tight clusters on the trunks of broadleaved trees, and successive crops may appear in the same place over the years. A delicious edible mushroom, it is best eaten when young, and has a pleasant 'mushroom' odour. The wide variation in colour, which can change from the young stage to the mature form, can make identification confusing, but the shell-shaped cap and white gills should be distinctive.

EATING

Excellent, often grown and sold commercially. Wild fruitbodies can have a tough skin, so only young specimens should be used; cook slowly. Tastes sweetish.

Habitat
On stumps and trunks of frondose trees, especially beech and poplar

LOOKALIKES

Blue oyster mushroom

Blue oyster mushroom
Pleurotus columbinus Very similar to the oyster but with a bluish cap. Edible.

Green oyster mushroom
Panellus serotinus A winter species, surviving early frosts. Cap olive green, slimy, gills yellow, crowded. Inedible.

Soft slipper toadstool
Crepidotus mollis One of the larger slipper toadstools, on dead branches, with white gills becoming cinnamon brown. Cap 2-7 cm in diameter, kidney-shaped, pale yellowish-brown, with an elastic pellicle; spore deposit snuff brown. Inedible, though not poisonous.

Soft slipper toadstool

Branched oyster mushroom

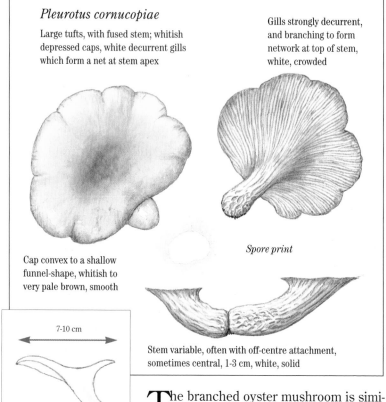

Pleurotus cornucopiae

Large tufts, with fused stem; whitish depressed caps, white decurrent gills which form a net at stem apex

Gills strongly decurrent, and branching to form network at top of stem, white, crowded

Cap convex to a shallow funnel-shape, whitish to very pale brown, smooth

Spore print

7-10 cm

Stem variable, often with off-centre attachment, sometimes central, 1-3 cm, white, solid

Flesh rather thin, soft, fleshy, white, with a smell either unpleasant or vaguely of aniseed

Frequency fairly common

Spore deposit white

The branched oyster mushroom is similar to the oyster mushroom (*Pleurotus ostreatus*) but the cap is more funnel-shaped as the stem is larger. It often has a compound structure, with the stems of the individual fruitbodies fusing at their base. It is commonly found in early autumn.

The central stem and sunken cap of this mushroom can lead to confusion with the funnel caps (*Clitocybe* species), but the fruitbody is much tougher and it always grows on dead wood.

EATING

Young specimens are edible, otherwise too tough.

Habitat
On stumps of
beech or elm

LOOKALIKES

Angels wings

Angels wings
Pleurocybella porrigens Often forms large
numbers of white clusters on dead conifer
stumps and roots, with fan-shaped, thin-
fleshed fruitbodies. Prefers colder localities,
in Britain limited to Scotland. Edible.

Veiled oyster
Pleurotus dryinus A large oyster, usually
solitary, and distinguished by the ring on the
stem and the yellowing gills. Edible when

young but developing a
firm to hard texture.

Cockle-shell wood cap
Lentinellus cochleatus
Fruitbodies, which dry
without rotting, are found
clustered on wood of
broadleaved trees. Cap
funnel-shaped, reddish
brown, gills narrow,
crowded. Edible when
young.

*Cockle-
shell wood
cap*

Split gill
Schizophyllum commune In warmer
regions, forming tiers of small, grey, hairy
brackets, with gills which appear to split
lengthwise, on stumps and trunks. Inedible.

King oyster mushroom

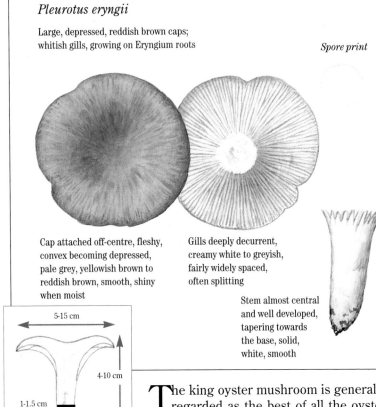

Pleurotus eryngii

Large, depressed, reddish brown caps;
whitish gills, growing on Eryngium roots

Spore print

Cap attached off-centre, fleshy,
convex becoming depressed,
pale grey, yellowish brown to
reddish brown, smooth, shiny
when moist

Gills deeply decurrent,
creamy white to greyish,
fairly widely spaced,
often splitting

Stem almost central
and well developed,
tapering towards
the base, solid,
white, smooth

5-15 cm

4-10 cm

1-1.5 cm

Flesh white, firm, lacking a
distinctive smell

Frequency rare, confined to
southern Europe

Spore deposit white

The king oyster mushroom is generally regarded as the best of all the oyster mushrooms. It is only found in southern European countries, growing on the roots of the Eryngo herb.

The variety *ferulae* forms clusters on several species of the umbellifers. It is now cultivated in some places, and so at times is available commercially.

Both the wild forms and the cultivated forms may be found for sale in the markets of southern Europe.

EATING

✗ ✗

Firm flesh with a sweet taste.

Habitat
Growing as a parasite on the roots of the larger plants of the carrot family (*Umbelliferae*), especially field eryngo (*Eryngium campestre*) and fennel (*Ferula*)

LOOKALIKES

Golden oyster
Pleurotus citrinopileatus Only found in supermarkets, grown commercially in the UK. Tufted, with up to 50 fruitbodies; cap 2-15 cm across, pure yellow, gills decurrent, cream, very crowded, short stem. On elm, in Russian Far East. Edible and decorative.

Pink oyster
Pleurotus salmoneostramineus Only found in supermarkets, grown commercially in UK. Similar to the oyster mushroom (*page 132*) but all parts are a beautiful salmon pink. Edible and decorative.

Hen of the woods

Grifola frondosa

Large clusters, on buried tree roots of ash or oak; caps small, greyish brown; pores whitish

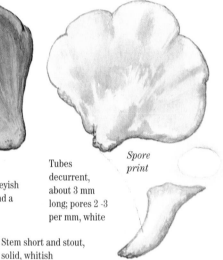

Cap fan-shaped and lobed, greyish brown, with radial streaks, and a thin, wavy edge

Tubes decurrent, about 3 mm long; pores 2 -3 per mm, white

Spore print

Stem short and stout, solid, whitish

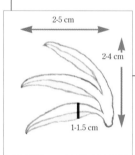

2-5 cm

2-4 cm

1-1.5 cm

Flesh thin, white, at first succulent then fibrous with either a sweetish smell, or an unpleasant odour when old

Frequency occasional, but occurs over several seasons in same locality

Spore deposit white

An annual species, only lasting for the season, but fresh fruitbodies are likely to reappear the following year. It forms large cauliflower-like clusters up to 30 cm across, with the individual stems joined to form a common base. More popular in North America and Japan, where it is known as 'mai-take'.

The umbrella polypore (*Polyporus umbellatus*) is similar, but has circular caps, each with a central stipe, and the entire fruitbody arises from an underground tuber.

EATING

Edible when young; too hard and fibrous when old.

Habitat
Tufted, growing from buried roots of deciduous trees, especially ash and oak

---

LOOKALIKES

Giant polypore
Meripilus giganteus Another compound bracket fungus, with much larger, shelf-like caps, 2-20 cm wide, greyish yellow, thick-fleshed, the pore surface bruises blackish, and the fairly short-lived fruitbody eventually blackens; mostly from roots and stumps of beech and oak. Eaten in North America.

Cauliflower fungus
Sparassis crispa A large yet delicate fungus resembling a whitish to cream cauliflower, with many short, flat, ribbon-like branches, it is found growing at the base of conifer stumps, especially pine. Edible. *See page 144.*

139

Chicken of the woods

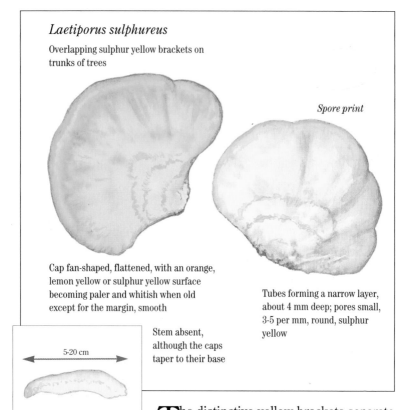

Laetiporus sulphureus

Overlapping sulphur yellow brackets on trunks of trees

Spore print

Cap fan-shaped, flattened, with an orange, lemon yellow or sulphur yellow surface becoming paler and whitish when old except for the margin, smooth

Tubes forming a narrow layer, about 4 mm deep; pores small, 3-5 per mm, round, sulphur yellow

Stem absent, although the caps taper to their base

5-20 cm

Flesh up to 5 cm thick, pale yellowish cream to almost white, at first soft and moist but becoming crumbly like chalk as it dries, developing a sour smell

Frequency common

Spore deposit white

The distinctive yellow brackets separate this species from other bracket fungi. It is widely eaten and extremely popular, especially in North America but there are confirmed reports that some people are allergic to it, suffering serious gastric upset and sometimes dizziness, on occasions within ten minutes of eating it. The alkaloids, hordenine, tyramine and N-methyltyramine are present, and apparently involved in the illness, although the precise mechanism remains unknown.

EATING

Often fried in breadcrumbs with mild taste, but sample only a very small portion when trying it for the first time and make sure only young, very fresh material is prepared. Do not eat raw.

Habitat
Clustered on trunks of living trees, preferring oak, sweet chestnut and yew; also reported on eucalyptus

LOOKALIKES

Dryad's saddle
Polyporus squamosus Cap up to 50 cm across, pale yellowish brown with blackish brown, fibrous scales and a lateral, short, black stem; pores large and angular; on higher branches of leafy trees, from early summer. Inedible.

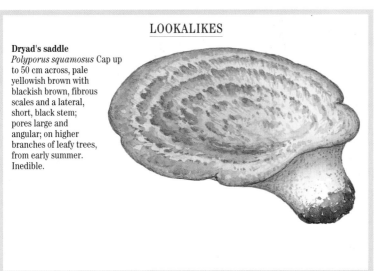

Beefsteak fungus

Fistulina hepatica

Reddish brown fleshy bracket, at base of oak or chestnut trunk; separate tubes in tube layer

Spore print

Cap bracket-shaped to tongue-like, with a pinkish to orange-red surface, sticky and finely warty

Stem absent, the cap tapering laterally to a thick point of attachment

Tube layer up to 1 cm deep, individual tubes separated from each other, opening by tiny pores, 2-3 per mm, at first whitish then yellowish, bruising reddish brown

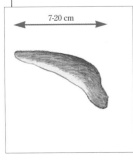

7-20 cm

Flesh 2-3 cm thick, at first soft, whitish or reddening, later fibrous and dry. No distinctive smell

Frequency occasional, more common in Britain and France than elsewhere in Europe

Spore deposit white

A peculiar fungus, unlikely to be confused, belonging to a family of its own. It is generally grouped among the 'polypores' owing to fine, vertical tubes under the cap, but on the beefsteak these are separated from each other, and represent elongations of minute, inverted cups. This is also known as 'oak tongue' and 'ox-tongue fungus' – it has the colour and texture of raw steak. Unpopular in forestry as it causes a brownish coloured rot, staining surrounding wood. However, 'brown oak' is sought after for making furniture.

EATING

The flavour is poor due to the presence of tannic acid, which it extracts from its host tree, resulting in a sour flavour. Before eating, parboil several times and discard the water. Older specimens are too dry and tough to eat.

Habitat
Singly on lower
branches and
stumps of old
oak and sweet
chestnut trees

LOOKALIKES

There are no close relatives or lookalikes to this fungus. Although apparently
similar to the bracket-like polypores, its affinity lies with a dissimilar group,
known as the *cyphellas*. If the lower pore surface is closely examined, it will be
seen that the many and crowded vertical tubes grow separately from each
other, not fused together. It is only found on large and old trees, and is the
main cause of decay of oak tree trunks, making them hollow.

Cauliflower fungus

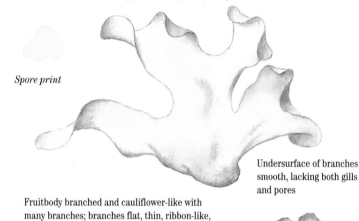

Sparassis crispa

Cauliflower-like, with curly, flat ribbons, whitish to yellowish

Spore print

Fruitbody branched and cauliflower-like with
many branches; branches flat, thin, ribbon-like,
1-2 cm broad, curly, wavy and leaf-like, pale
cream to pale yellow, at times growing together;
arising from a stalk-like base

Undersurface of branches
smooth, lacking both gills
and pores

Stem short, mostly
buried, solid, white,
blackening with age

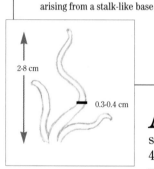

2-8 cm

0.3-0.4 cm

Flesh white, thin, tough; with
a sweetish aromatic smell

Frequency occasional to
locally common

Spore deposit cream colour

Also known as the brain fungus, this is a
root parasite of pines, growing on
stumps or nearby. The fruitbodies can reach
40 cm across. It makes good eating and dries
well – so it is a shame that it is not more
common. Fruitbodies often occur over several seasons of the year.

Even more uncommon related species
include *Sparassis laminosa*, which is less
branched, with flatter lobes, and usually
grows with either beech or oak, and
Sparassis simplex, with a single lobe.

EATING

Highly regarded, with a mild taste, but must first be
thoroughly washed. Discard old specimens.

144

Habitat
On stumps and
at base of
conifers,
especially pine

LOOKALIKES

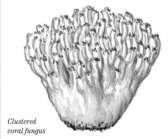

*Clustered
coral fungus*

Clustered coral fungus
Ramaria botrytis Uncommon, occurs in
rainy years. Fruitbodies up to 15 cm across,
white to yellowish, with thick base and many
short branches with wine red tips; on ground
in beech woods. Edible, except for the bitter
tips.

**White coral
fungus**
*Clavulina
cristata* Common
and often found in
large numbers in
woodland. Small fruitbodies uniformly white,
highly branched, with crested tips.
Edible, but not recommended.

*White coral
fungus*

Hen of the woods
Grifola frondosa A compound 'polypore'
with small caps on short stems; each cap
has a pore layer. *See page 138.*

Morels, truffles and cup fungi

These three groups differ widely in their form and behaviour. The morels resemble mushrooms to the extent that they have a cap borne upon a central stem, whilst the cup fungi, as the name suggests, are cup- or saucer-shaped and rarely have a stem. The truffles form solid, round balls, which grow underground. Nevertheless, all belong to the same class, the Ascomycetes, which is the largest of the classes and quite distinct from the class Basidiomycetes, to which the mushrooms and toadstools belong.

Morels are springtime fungi, usually occurring from April through to June, although each crop will only survive for several days. As few other mushrooms are available at that time of year, morels are highly prized. They prefer a disturbed soil, and are especially common in old apple orchards, under hedgerows, on wasteland, composted areas, and sites of forest fires. There are several species, but all may be recognized by the sponge-like, honeycombed or ridged cap. The difference between the species has proved difficult to define, but the best known is the **common morel** (*Morchella esculenta*, page 148), also known as the yellow morel.

Common morel

There are about 30 species of the true truffles (*Tuber* species), although there are many similar fungi which also grow underground. The fruitbody is ball-shaped and solid, and when it is cut open the flesh reveals a marbled appearance. The spores are produced within the fruitbody and only discharged when the fruitbody either disintegrates or is eaten by a passing animal. They have evolved an underground life-style to gain protection from drying out, and therefore they can survive longer than a typical mushroom.

Truffles may be found throughout Europe but become much scarcer in northerly localities. The main truffle-producing area lies between 40-47° latitude or the Mediterranean region. The climate and soil requirements are very precise for each stage of the life-cycle. Soil must preferably be well-drained, light, slightly alkaline or chalky, and never a heavy clay soil.

To find truffles, it is necessary to detect their distinctive scent. Traditionally, a pig was used, but increasingly dogs, which are easier to control, have taken over. Truffles may also be detected by small cracks appearing in the top soil or by the hovering presence of the truffle fly.

The best known of the truffles is undoubtedly the **Périgord truffle** (*Tuber melanosporum*, page 150), also known as the black truffle. Attempts at artificial cultivation have been made, with some success in France in the 1960s, and more recently in New

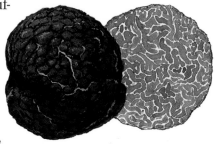

Périgord truffle

Zealand. The Périgord truffle is virtually always associated with oak trees, and commercial production has involved inoculating the surrounding soil with soil taken from known truffle trees, or by transferring saplings. The fruitbodies take 7-15 years to produce by this method. More widespread, but generally regarded as much inferior in taste, is another black truffle, the **summer truffle** (*Tuber aestivum,* page 151). This is also known as the 'English truffle', and was collected commercially in England up to 1935.

Gastronomically, the cup fungi compare neither to morels nor truffles, and many are suspected of causing monomethylhydrazine poisoning, like the **turban fungus (***Gyromitra esculenta,* page 149**)**. An exception, however, is the **orange peel** (*Aleuria aurantia,* page 154), one of the few edible fungi that is consumed in the raw state.

Orange peel

Common morel

Morchella esculenta

Head with deep polygonal cavities; hollow stem; appears in spring

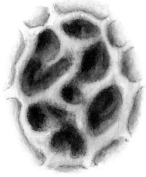

Spore print

Cap variable in form, from almost spherical to ovoid or conical, yellow, yellowish brown to blackish brown, and bearing deep ridges with cross walls to give a honeycomb-like appearance of polygonal cavities, hollow

Stem about same length as the cap height; white to ochre yellow, smooth or scurfy, sometimes ribbed or wrinkled, hollow

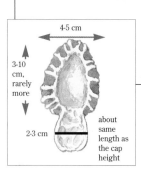

4-5 cm

3-10 cm, rarely more

2-3 cm

about same length as the cap height

Flesh thin, whitish, brittle, with a fungoid smell

Frequency occasional or locally common in season

Spore deposit ochre yellow

Once established, the morel often reappears at the same site for many years. It is much prized as a springtime fungus and for its eating qualities. There are a number of varieties, varying in shape and colour: yellow, with a round, large head (var. *rigida*); ochre yellow and small (var. *rotunda*); greyish brown to ochre yellow, with a rounded to conical head (var. *vulgaris*); blackish brown, with a rounded to conical head (var. *umbrina*). Avoid confusion with the poisonous turban fungus or 'false morel'.

EATING

Excellent, with a mild taste, after slow cooking. Fruitbodies can be dried for later use, or powdered as a seasoning. Must not be eaten raw.

Habitat
On bare, sandy ground, under hedgerows, on embankments and roadsides, generally where there is little competition, usually in groups, sometimes in very large numbers

LOOKALIKES

Turban fungus
Gyromitra esculenta A conifer-wood species, especially under pines and spruce, having a much-lobed, brain-like, reddish brown cap and short, whitish stalk. Poisonous; deadly if eaten raw and sometimes harmful even after cooking. *See page 178.*

Turban fungus

Common white saddle
Helvella crispa Common species with a whitish, convoluted, saddle-shaped cap, 2-5 cm across, and deeply furrowed, whitish stalk; in woodlands from July to October. Edible but worthless.

Common white saddle

Elfin saddle
Helvella lacunosa Similar in form, but has dark grey or blackish cap and stem, and lobes of the cap attached to the stem in places.

Périgord truffle

Tuber melanosporum

Hard, black ball with pyramidal warts; flesh greyish changing to reddish and finally black; strong pungent odour; underground

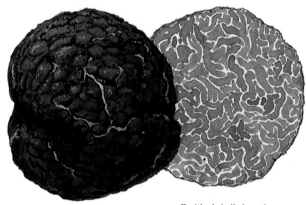

Fruitbody ball-shaped, sometimes flattened or knobbly, with a reddish to dull black surface bearing numerous small, pyramidal warts

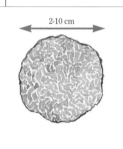

2-10 cm

Flesh solid, at first grey then reddish violet, finally black, marbled with white veins which blush reddish, with a strong pungent smell

Frequency common in southern France, Spain, Italy

Spore deposit dark brown

Also called the black truffle, this is the best known of all the truffles, which are the most prized of edible mushrooms. They grow underground and are hunted by dogs or pigs who can scent their odour. The Périgord truffle occurs only in Mediterranean countries, and is a major industry in southern France, Spain and Italy. The bagnoli truffle (*Tuber mesentericum*), which is hollow, and Bourgoyne truffle (*T. uncinatium*), dark maroon in colour, are closely related and very popular in France.

EATING

Edible with a pungent, unique aroma, usually grated; can be boiled, roasted or preserved in oil. The flavour is volatile, and best cooked simply and quickly, such as coarsely grated into an omelette.

Habitat
Grows under oak trees, occasionally chestnut or hazel, about 3-20 cm deep in alkaline soil

LOOKALIKES

Summer truffle

Hart's truffle

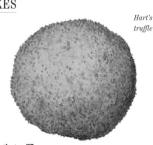

Summer truffle
Tuber aestivum Grows in chalky soil, often associated with beech trees; fairly common in Britain, formerly collected by professional truffle hunters. Fruitbody 3-9 cm across, blackish brown, with prominent wart-like scales; flesh at first whitish becoming olive brown, and marbled with white veins. Smell and flavour milder than Périgord truffle.

Hart's truffle
Elaphomyces granulatus An underground truffle, widespread in both leafy and conifer woods, sometimes found on the surface amongst leaf litter. About 4 cm across, yellowish brown with granular surface, flesh pinkish buff developing a black, powdery spore mass. Inedible.

151

White Piedmont truffle

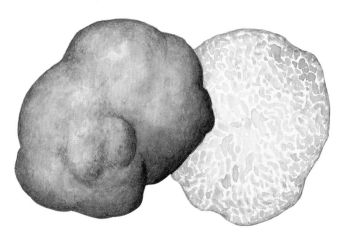

Tuber magnatum

Resembes a knobbly potato, grows underground; strong aromatic smell

Fruitbody rather irregular in form resembling a potato, often knobbly, yellowish-brown, smooth, or somewhat cracking

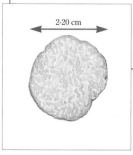

2-20 cm

Flesh greyish pink, marbled with white veins, with a strong and intense aroma

Frequency rare and localized

Spore deposit dark brown

A truffle (see also page 146) is any fungus which grows underground. This one is found only in Italy, where it is known as the famous *'tartufo bianco di Alba'* – and as the 'king of the truffles'. It is confined to the north of the country, occurring in parts of Piedmont, Umbria, Emilia-Romagna and Tuscany. Weight for weight, this is one of the world's most expensive foods. The high price is on account of its rarity, the difficulty in finding it, and the fact that it cannot be cultivated.

EATING

Strong and intense flavour; eaten grated with pasta.

Habitat
Underground, in association with oaks, possibly also poplars

LOOKALIKES

White truffle
Choiromyces meandriformis Found throughout Europe, including Britain and Scandinavia, amongst leaf mould in mixed woods. Irregular and knobbly, 3-8 cm, rarely, 12 cm across, with a thin, smooth, whitish skin, and a white, marbled flesh with grey veins. Not edible except when powdered and used as a spice, and then highly valued.

Orange peel

Aleuria aurantia

Irregular cup-shape with orange inner surface

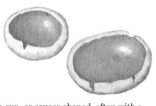

Cap cup- or saucer-shaped, often with a wavy edge, with a bright orange, smooth, inner (fertile) surface and a pale creamy white, powdery, outer surface; lacking a stem

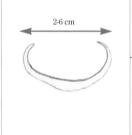

2-6 cm

Flesh thin, watery-white, brittle, with a scarcely noticeable smell

Frequency common

Spore deposit white

Its brilliant orange colour distinguishes this species from all others, and means that it can easily be mistaken for discarded orange peel. Although there are many cup fungi, some relatively large, this is one of the few that are regarded as edible. The fruitbodies usually appear in clusters.

Like all cup fungi, the orange peel's fertile layer, which produces the spores, is on the upper (inner) surface, and the mature spores can sometimes be seen puffed out as a cloud.

EATING	
	A weak taste – needs to be well cooked.

Habitat
On hard or disturbed, sandy soil, often on embankments or roadsides, sometimes in large troops

LOOKALIKES

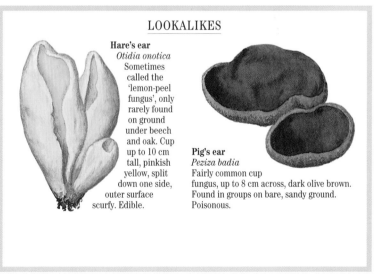

Hare's ear
Otidia onotica
Sometimes called the 'lemon-peel fungus', only rarely found on ground under beech and oak. Cup up to 10 cm tall, pinkish yellow, split down one side, outer surface scurfy. Edible.

Pig's ear
Peziza badia
Fairly common cup fungus, up to 8 cm across, dark olive brown. Found in groups on bare, sandy ground. Poisonous.

Jelly fungi

Jelly leaf

Most jelly fungi are edible but tasteless. Some species, such as mo-ehr (*Auricularia polytricha*) and silver ears (*Tremella fuciformis*), are grown commercially on a very large scale throughout the Far East, and were amongst the first fungi in history to be cultivated.

The jelly fungi represent a mixed group, with species belonging to many families, but all possess the common feature of a gelatinized flesh, which will dry down, sometimes to a fine, transparent film but when moistened will swell into a fleshy fruitbody. Although there is little in the way of taste, the attraction lies in their texture, together with their ability to be kept for long periods once dried.

The fruitbodies can vary considerably both in form and colour. Some species, such as *Tremella* and *Exidia*, may be flat and disk-like or wrinkled and brain-like, whilst the jelly antler fungi (*Calocera* species) are club- or coral-shaped.

The most distinctive group and the one most frequently put to culinary use is the wood ears (*Auricularia* species). The common European species is the **Jew's ear** (*Auricularia auricula-judae*, page 158), the name being a corruption of Judas's ear, reflecting an old fable that Judas hanged himself from an elder tree. The species is mostly found on old elder, although it does also occur on other trees, such as oak and sycamore. In North America, it is known as the 'tree ear'. The fruitbody more or less resembles a human ear, and is attached to the bark by one side, growing out in clusters. It is rubbery to the touch when moist. This species is closely related and very similar to the mo-ehr, which has a more velvety outer surface.

Oppostie *Jew's ears*

Jew's ear

Auricularia auricula-judae

Approximate size and shape
of a human ear; jelly-like

Fertile surface (inner)
greyish brown, usually
wrinkled or veined,
otherwise smooth and shiny

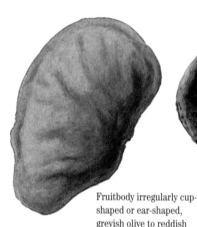
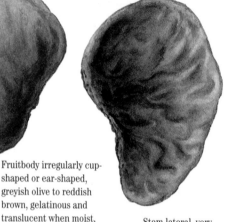

Fruitbody irregularly cup-
shaped or ear-shaped,
greyish olive to reddish
brown, gelatinous and
translucent when moist,
laterally attached, the
outer surface appearing
finely powdery, with very
short, greyish hairs

Stem lateral, very
short or absent,
narrow

3-10 cm

Flesh thin, rubbery, slightly
translucent, swollen when
wet, drying hard and horny;
lacking any smell

Frequency common

Spore deposit white

This strange-looking, yet easily recognizable mushroom grows on the branches
of several species of tree, particularly elder
and sycamore. The fruitbody is gelatinous
or rubbery to the touch, and usually grows
in clusters. It is closely related and very similar to the Mo-Ehr (*Auricularia polytricha*)
which is commercially grown in the Far
East and extensively exported. The Jew's
ear is widely used in stir-fry dishes and
soups in Chinese cuisine, probably more for
its chewy texture than its flavour.

EATING

✗

Little or no taste. Usually cut into small pieces and
cooked gently in stews and casseroles. Dries well and is
readily reconstituted.

Habitat
Clustered on dead branches, especially of elder and elm, preferring damp. warm localities

LOOKALIKES

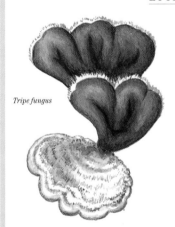

Tripe fungus

Tripe fungus
Auricularia mesenterica A common species distinguished by the gelatinous, bracket-like fruitbodies which have a densely hairy upper surface with alternating zones of grey and brown. The fertile (lower) surface is reddish purple, smooth or veined; on stumps and logs of leafy trees, especially elm. Not edible.

Silver leaf fungus
Chondrostereum purpureum Has similar, shaggy brackets and purplish fertile surface, but is not gelatinous. Weakly parasitic, a disease of plum trees, causing the leaves to turn silver. Inedible.

Jelly leaf

Tremella foliacea

Brownish, leaf-like
lobes; jelly-like texture

Fertile surface
smooth, covering the
whole of the lobes

Fruitbody gelatinous
throughout, brownish or
flesh-coloured, comprising
flattened, leaf-like lobes
which arise from a short,
wrinkled, common base

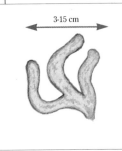

3-15 cm

Flesh thin, only 1 mm or so in
thickness, soft, translucent
and colourless; no odour

Frequency occasional

Spore deposit white

Probably the largest of the European jelly fungi. Not generally eaten, but harmless. All *Tremella* species dry down to a thin, brittle membrane in dry weather, becoming jelly-like after rain. Closely related to silver ears (*Tremella fuciformis*), the jelly leaf is cultivated in China and is the only fungus that can be used as a dessert. The brittle flesh is broken into small pieces and served in a bowl of sugar water – apparently a refreshing dish. The Chinese believe that it has a number of therapeutic properties.

EATING

Edible, but lacking any flavour. Can be dried, and
reconstituted after soaking, when added to soups and
stews.

Habitat
On dead
branches and
logs of
coniferous and
deciduous trees

LOOKALIKES

Black witch's butter
Exidia glandulosa At first cushion-shaped
becoming brain-like with small, wavy folds,
10-30 cm, black, gelatinous, smooth and
shiny; dries to a thin membrane; on dead
wood of leafy trees, irregularly spread over
the substratum. Inedible.

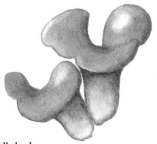

Jelly knob
Tremiscus helvelloides Growing in clusters,
with flattened, wavy, gelatinous caps, 3-10 cm
high, tapering to a stalk-like base, salmon
pink to reddish brown; on the ground in shady
places, usually on buried wood. Inedible.

Poisonous mushrooms:
an introduction

It has been said that all mushrooms are edible but some only once. It is essential, therefore, that the mushroom enthusiast knows which species may be eaten without fear. There are about three to four thousand species of mushrooms growing in Europe. Only around 250 to 300 known to be, or are suspected of being, toxic. However, this is a far higher figure than that given for the number of known edible species.

It is important to be clear about what is meant by mushroom poisoning. A few individuals are intolerant to normal, edible species, such as the cultivated mushroom (*Agaricus bisporus*), and suffer stomach upset after eating it. This is not generally regarded as mushroom poisoning. Symptoms of toxicity can also result from eating too many mushrooms, or from imaginary poisonings. The hyphal walls (see page 8) of all fungi are largely composed of chitin, which is difficult to digest. Individuals with weak digestion may suffer as the result of too much chitin. Others can mistakenly believe themselves to be poisoned from a mushroom dish, with psychosomatic symptoms, including gastric disturbance, sweating and palpitations, that simulate a real case of poisoning.

There are some obvious rules for anyone who wants to eat wild mushrooms. The first is to learn the toxic species. Find these out from an expert but be sure that he/she is really an expert. Correct identification is not easy and caution must always be exercised. There are no foolproof methods for identifying poisonous species. Secondly, learn the anatomy of a mushroom, so that you know how to look for the ring, and the volva, the possible colour variations, and the different stages of mushroom growth.

Remember that life-threatening poisonings are rare, and even in cases which are potentially fatal, the illness will be spread over a period, allowing time for treatment. Should symptoms occur after a meal:

1 Get immediate medical assistance. If there is a delay in the onset of symptoms for six to ten hours or more, go straight to hospital.
2 Vomiting should be induced, unless the individual is unconscious, to eliminate any toxin as quickly as possible. This is done by tickling the back of the throat. Use of a strong saline solution is not generally recommended. A bland drink, such as milk or water, may then be given to dilute any remaining toxins.
3 Retain all evidence of the fungus consumed. This might include any regurgitated material, so that a professional mycologist has a chance of identifying the mushroom.

4 Be prepared to answer questions about the mushroom. These may include information about its appearance and occurrence, as well as its condition, storage, preparation and cooking.

If you are trying a wild 'edible mushroom' for the first time, then
a) Take only a small amount.
b) Retain at least one fruitbody, in case it is needed for identification.
c) Do not mix different species.

True mushroom poisonings are referred to as mycetisms. Most poisonings usually result from mistaking a poisonous species for an edible one. Increasingly, however, poisonings result from eating species with psychotropic or intoxicating properties, for so-called recreational purposes. Mycetisms are different from mycoses, which are brought about by the effect of the parasitic growth of fungi, usually moulds or yeasts, within or on the human body. Similarly, mycotoxicosis is brought about by the production of toxic compounds from the action of moulds which grow on old or decayed mushrooms.

Not all poisonings are the same, and the various types, identified by typical sets of symptoms are called syndromes. The major groups, introduced separately in the sections that follow, are:

1 Cell-damaging mushrooms: *See pages 164-179.*
2 Blood cell-damaging mushrooms: *See pages 180-185.*
3 Hallucinogenic mushrooms and alcohol-related poisoning: *See pages 186-187.*
4 Sweat-inducing mushrooms: *See pages 198-209.*
5 Ibotenic acid poisoning: *See pages 210-215.*
6 Digestive system irritants: *See pages 216-237.*
7 Allergies and contamination: *See pages 238-239.*

Finally, it is worth knowing that certain fleshy mushrooms can selectively absorb trace elements, such as vanadium and rubidium, and heavy metals from the soil. Some puffballs and *Agaricus* species have been shown to accumulate toxic metals, such as mercury and cadmium, and zinc is also taken up. Surveys throughout Europe, following the Chernobyl accident in 1989, have revealed concentrations of radio-caesium (^{137}Cs) in wild, fleshy mushrooms. It is a wise precaution not to collect edible mushrooms in heavily industrialized sites, by roadsides or in car parks. Equally, avoid mushroom areas where pesticides, fungicides and weedkillers have been used.

Cell-damaging mushrooms

There are three different types of toxins involved

Cyclopeptides
These are by far the most serious causes of poisoning, accounting for more than 90 per cent of all deaths from mushroom poisoning worldwide. A large number of cyclopeptides have been extracted from species of *Amanita*, resulting in nine amatoxins (bicyclic octapeptides), seven phallotoxins (bicyclic heptapeptides) and seven virotoxins (monocyclic heptapeptides).

The phallotoxins were the first to be isolated from the **death cap** (*Amanita phalloides*, page 166), and were thought to be the cause of the poisoning, but it is now known that the amatoxins are the active compounds. Amatoxins are amongst the most toxic substances known. The organs attacked are those generally concerned with protein synthesis, especially the liver, but also the kidneys, pancreas and the superficial layer of the gut. Technically, amatoxins interfere with RNA and DNA transcription by inhibiting the enzyme RNA polymerase.

Death cap

The symptoms show four more or less distinct phases:

1 Latent phase, with no apparent effects from six to 24 hours.
2 Gastric phase, with vomiting and diarrhoea, resulting in dehydration and electrolyte disturbances.
3 A short period of apparent well-being, and
4 Hepatic phase, occurring 36 to 48 hours after ingestion, developing jaundice and acute hepatic failure. Death can occur within six to 18 days. Treatment involves emetics, repeated dosages of activated charcoal, rehydration, and careful monitoring of the hepatic functioning. The severity of the poisoning will depend upon the amount of mushroom consumed and the delay in treatment. A specific antidote for cyclopeptide poisoning still proves to be difficult and remains unresolved, although liver transplantation has proved successful.

Most poisonings have involved the *Amanita* species, which have been mistaken either for true mushrooms (*Agaricus* species) or, when small, unopened fruitbodies, for puffballs. Other mushrooms causing cytolytic poisoning include the **destroying angel** (*Amanita virosa,* page 168), the **spring Amanita** (*Amanita vernia,* page 170), the **marginate pixy cap** (*Galerina marginata,* page 172), and a number of *Lepiota* species (page 174).

Orellanin

Species of the web caps (*Cortinarius*) were considered edible until the 1950s, when several reports appeared, especially from Poland, of poisoning. The mushroom involved became known as the Poznan web cap (*Cortinarius orellanus*, see page 176), and the active compound has been identified as a complex of five cyclopeptides. Remarkably, and unfortunately, there is a long latent period, from 36 hours to 11 days before the symptoms show up. These include a severe burning thirst, leading eventually to chronic kidney failure. Some patients have recovered after about six days, but otherwise renal dialysis is required, and eventually, kidney transplantation.

There are several hundred species of web caps, of which many are hardly known. So avoid all the species in this genus. The species are characteristic in having a brown spore deposit and in the earlier stages, before the cap has fully expanded, there is a cobweb-like veil (called a cortina) under the cap which protects the young gills. Most of the species which are known to contain orellanin have bright orange-brown caps with a raised centre, and are collectively fairly easy to recognize.

Monomethylhydrazine

The number of cases of monomethylhydrazine poisoning in Europe exceeds that of *Amanita* poisoning, almost entirely due to the **turban fungus** (*Gyromitra esculenta*, page 178), being mistaken for edible morels. The toxin, gyromitrin, is found in varying amounts in different fruitbodies, collected in different areas, so that there is variation in the degree of toxicity reported. Sometimes recovery of a patient occurs within six days; in other cases, acute hepatitis can lead to death. Gyromitrin is hydrolysed within the body to form monomethylhydrazine, a substance which interferes with vitamin B utilization. Again, there is a latent period, delaying the onset of symptoms from six to 12 hours. The symptoms include nausea, headaches, cramp, jaundice and coma.

Death cap

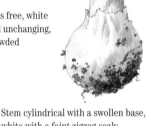
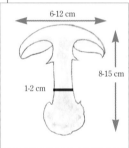

Along with the destroying angel, (page 168), this is the most deadly mushroom, all the more dangerous because it can be mistaken for edible true mushrooms (*Agaricus* species). Be alert for the volva, white gills (never becoming pinkish or chocolate brown), and an unpleasant smell. A single mushroom can be fatal, and it is deadly whether raw or cooked. Wash your hands after picking. Never mix with other mushrooms. In Britain, it is mainly confined to England and Wales.

Poisoning attacks the liver, kidneys, and digestive system. Vomiting and diarrhoea start six hours after eating, followed by a short remission, then jaundice and liver failure after 36 to 48 hours.

Habitat
Leafy woods,
often oak,
sometimes
conifers; in the
autumn months

LOOKALIKES

Field mushroom
Agaricus campestris Pale forms of death cap
could be confused; note the gills are pink
becoming chocolate brown, and there is
never any development of a volva at stem
base. *See page 36.*

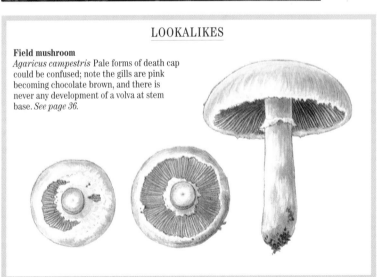

Destroying angel

Amanita virosa

Entirely white; cap smooth, stem scaly, curved, with ring and volva; strong, unpleasant smell

Cap at first conical and only rarely fully expanding, with a raised centre, white, shiny, smooth, sticky when moist

Gills free, white, crowded

Spore print

Stem slender and often slightly curved, covered with loose, woolly scales, together with a large, white, membranous ring and a cup-like volva at the base

6-18 cm

8-15 cm

1-1.5 cm

Flesh fairly thin, soft, fleshy.

Frequency rare to occasional

Spore deposit pure white

As poisonous as the death cap (*Amanita phalloides*, page 168), with many deaths recorded in Europe, although it generally grows in northerly or higher altitudes. Although normally rare, in some years this species can occur in quantities. In Britain, it is virtually confined to Scotland, and never common. Neither this, nor the death cap grows in open grassland. Even experts can confuse it with young, white true mushrooms (*Agaricus* species), particularly in the button stage. Examine the stem carefully, looking for a ring and a volva. The distinctive smell, especially of old specimens, is likened to bad perfume or just plain stinking. Causes vomiting and diarrhoea after six hours, before jaundice and liver failure after 36-48 hours.

Habitat
Leafy and mixed
woods, often
under beech

LOOKALIKES

Grisette
Amanita vaginata
The grisettes differ
from other Amanita species in the
absence of a ring on the stem but they do
retain the volva at the base. Edible when
fully cooked but poisonous raw. *See pages
100 and 184.*

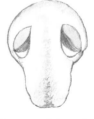

Cross sections of the unopened stages of
an *Amanita* species, above left, showing
a ring and basal volva; and a true
mushroom (*Agaricus*) species, above
right, showing a ring only.

Spring Amanita

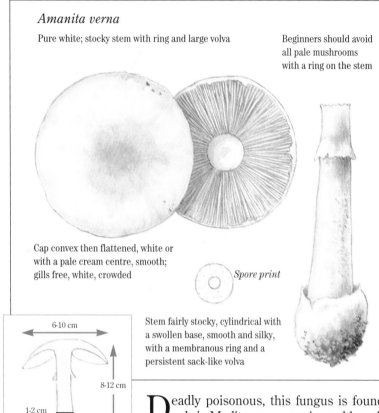

Amanita verna

Pure white; stocky stem with ring and large volva

Beginners should avoid all pale mushrooms with a ring on the stem

Cap convex then flattened, white or with a pale cream centre, smooth; gills free, white, crowded

Spore print

Stem fairly stocky, cylindrical with a swollen base, smooth and silky, with a membranous ring and a persistent sack-like volva

6-10 cm

8-12 cm

1-2 cm

Flesh thin and white

Frequency occasional, but confined to Mediterranean areas

Spore deposit white

Deadly poisonous, this fungus is found only in Mediterranean regions; although recorded in Britain, it is probably confused with pale forms of the false death cap. Contrary to its popular name, it appears in late summer rather than spring. Unlike the other poisonous *Amanita* species, it lacks any discernible smell. It is easily confused with edible true mushrooms *(Agaricus* species) but the gills stay white – never pink, brown or blackish. It is also similar to the smooth Lepiota *(Leucoagaricus naucinus)*, but distinguished by the large, white volva. Very closely related to the death cap *(Amanita phalloides*, page 166), and may have a pale greenish tint at the centre of cap. Stomach upset occurs six hours after eating.

Habitat
In both leafy and coniferous woodland

LOOKALIKES

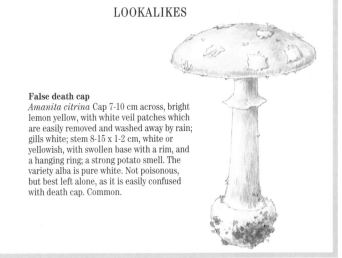

False death cap
Amanita citrina Cap 7-10 cm across, bright lemon yellow, with white veil patches which are easily removed and washed away by rain; gills white; stem 8-15 x 1-2 cm, white or yellowish, with swollen base with a rim, and a hanging ring; a strong potato smell. The variety alba is pure white. Not poisonous, but best left alone, as it is easily confused with death cap. Common.

Marginate pixy cap

Galerina marginata

Small brown tufts on dead conifer wood; brown gills, fibrous ring on stem

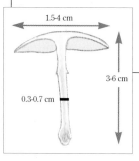

Cap convex, eventually flattened, yellowish tawny brown with slightly paler margin, then drying to buff; striated when moist

Gills adnate, pale brown to tawny brown, crowded

Stem cylindrical yellowish brown, darker below, with a small but persistent ring on upper part

1.5-4 cm

3-6 cm

0.3-0.7 cm

Spore print

Flesh thin, pale, with a floury smell

Frequency common

Spore deposit rust brown

Many small, brown mushrooms are confusing and difficult to identify, and this is one of the few that are deadly poisonous. It contains amatoxins, similar to those of the death cap (*Amanita phalloides*, page 166), and related species.

Most of the deaths it causes arise from confusion with other species, especially the two-toned scale head (page 60), which is more robust, with a scaly stem, and even with the hallucinogenic liberty caps (*Psilocybe semilanceata*, page 188), which lack a ring and grow amongst grass. Always look for the ring on the stem and note that it only lives on dead wood. Owing to the toxity of this species, it is best to always avoid small brown mushrooms.

Habitat
On stumps and dead branches of conifer trees

LOOKALIKES

Deadly pixy cap
Galerina autumnalis Cap 1-3 cm across, convex then flattened, thin-fleshed, dark brown drying to pale brown, smooth, slightly sticky, with a striated edge; gills adnate, narrow, cinnamon brown, moderately crowded; stem 2-6 x 0.2-0.4 cm, dark brown, with a membranous ring; flesh thin, brown; spore deposit brown; on fallen branches of ash, birch, beech, oak.

Thread cone cap
Conocybe filaris Cap 1-3 cm across, conical, expanding, reddish brown, drying yellow ochre, with a faintly striated margin; gills adnexed, ochre brown; stem 4-5 x 0.2-0.3 cm, whitish, finely powdery, with a white, membranous ring midway up the stem; spore deposit brown; in grassy places and on roadsides. Deadly; several similar species are probably equally toxic.

Deadly Lepiota

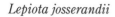

Lepiota josserandii

Cap and stem with loose pinkish scales;
ring on stem, whitish gills

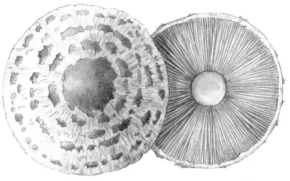

Cap convex, covered with concentric
rings of pinkish ochre to pinkish grey
scales on a pale ground

Gills free, white to
pinkish, crowded

Spore print

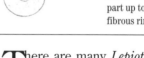

Stem cylindrical,
white to pinkish,
with indefinite
scales on lower
part up to a
fibrous ring-zone

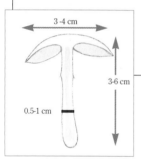

3 -4 cm

3-6 cm

0.5-1 cm

Flesh thin, pinkish, with an
aromatic, fruity smell

Frequency occasional

Spore deposit white

There are many *Lepiota* species, mostly small with scaly caps, pale gills, and a ring on the stem. Avoid them: they contain deadly amatoxins.

The group includes: the rusty brown Lepiota and rusty pink Lepiota (see opposite); the black scaly Lepiota (*Lepiota felina*), which has blackish scales on cap and stem, smells of pelargonium, and is found under conifers; the pinkish parasol (*Lepiota subincarnata*) with pink to pinkish brown flesh, scales on cap and stem, and a scarcely-developed ring; *Lepiota fulvella* – reddish-brown scales, banded stem, found on disturbed soil; whilst *Lepiota pseudohelveola* has dark, pinkish brown scales, a ring with a brown edge, and a fruity smell.

Habitat
On the ground
in fields,
gardens, parks

LOOKALIKES

*Rusty
brown
Lepiota*

**Rusty brown
Lepiota**
*Lepiota
brunneoincarnata* Cap
with pinkish brown scales
in zones and a blackish
centre, found in sandy
woodland but also on
lawns. One of the more
robust species and fairly
common. Deadly.

*Rusty pink
Lepiota*

Rusty pink Lepiota
Lepiota helveola Cap
covered with pinkish
brown scales, with a
vinaceous brown centre.
Stem has a zigzag
pattern. Faint smell.
Prefers warm locations.
Deadly.

Chestnut parasol
Lepiota castanea Cap with small, brown,
fibrous scales on a pale yellow ground; stem
3-4 x 0.2-0.4 cm, covered with small, brown,
fibrous scales below ring; in both leafy and
coniferous woods, and by roadsides. Deadly.

Foxy-orange web cap

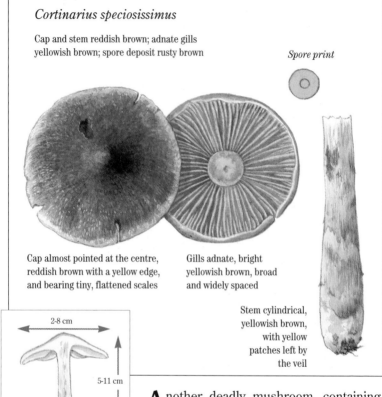

Cortinarius speciosissimus

Cap and stem reddish brown; adnate gills
yellowish brown; spore deposit rusty brown

Spore print

Cap almost pointed at the centre,
reddish brown with a yellow edge,
and bearing tiny, flattened scales

Gills adnate, bright
yellowish brown, broad
and widely spaced

Stem cylindrical,
yellowish brown,
with yellow
patches left by
the veil

2-8 cm

5-11 cm

0.5-1 cm

Flesh firm, yellowish, with a
smell of radish

Frequency rare in northern
Europe; more common further
south

Spore deposit rusty brown

Another deadly mushroom, containing
orellanin, which results in kidney failure,
with a delayed reaction time of two weeks or
more. The Poznan web cap (*Cortinarius orellanus*) is similar but found under oaks in acid
soils. Other web caps also contain orellanin,
so it is wise to avoid this group altogether.
Most of them are very difficult to identify, in
any case.

The reddish to yellowish brown colours of
this species should be distinctive, but recently pickers have mistaken it for the golden yellow chanterelle. It is essential to look for the
cobweb veil and brown spore deposit.

Symptoms include headache, intense
thirst and shivering, but no high temperature. Loss of kidney function follows.

Habitat
On the ground, in small groups in conifer woods

LOOKALIKES

Deadly web cap
Cortinarius gentilis Cap ochre yellow to orange, felty; gills ochraceous to yellowish brown; stem ochre yellow with bright yellow patches of veil remnants; in conifer woods, especially spruce. Deadly.

Chanterelle
Cantharellus cibarius All parts egg yellow to yellow ochre; gills replaced with thick, branching ridges with decurrent attachment; spore deposit pale, not brown. *See page 24*

Turban fungus

Gyromitra esculenta

Brain-like convoluted
cap on short stem

Cap more or less spherical,
convoluted and brain-like,
yellowish brown to blackish
brown, with the margin
rolled inwards

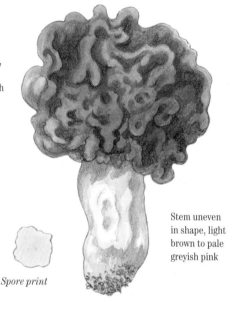

Stem uneven
in shape, light
brown to pale
greyish pink

Spore print

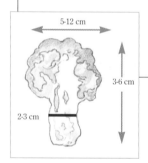

5-12 cm

3-6 cm

2-3 cm

Flesh thin, brittle, with a
pleasant smell

Frequency occasional to
common, preferring northerly
localities

Spore deposit ochre yellow

Also known as the false morel, the turban
fungus can be abundant in Scandinavia,
growing on disturbed, sandy soil in spruce
forests.

It causes poisonings throughout Europe,
generally when mistaken for the common
morel (page 148). It appears to contain the
toxin gyromitrin in varying amounts – sometimes the fungus is eaten without ill-effects.
The poison can be removed by repeatedly
parboiling for ten minutes at a time and discarding the water.

Gyromitrin is a cell-destroyer. Symptoms
start six to 12 hours after eating, and include
exhaustion, stomach pains, continuous vomiting and leg cramps. Recovery is after two to
six days.

178

Habitat
In conifer woods

LOOKALIKES

Hooded saddle
Gyromitra infula Cap 3-10 cm across, lobed, saddle-shaped, convoluted, reddish to dark brown; stem whitish, amongst woody debris; June to October. Poisonous.

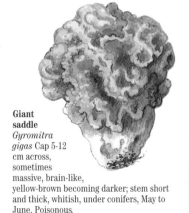

Giant saddle
Gyromitra gigas Cap 5-12 cm across, sometimes massive, brain-like, yellow-brown becoming darker; stem short and thick, whitish, under conifers, May to June. Poisonous.

Blood cell-damaging mushrooms (haemolytic poisoning)

There are a large number of mushrooms which, when well cooked, can be eaten safely and cause no harmful effects. However, when these same species are consumed in the raw state some discomfort and, in rare instances, serious illness can result. As a precaution, raw mushrooms should only ever be consumed in small amounts, and this advice becomes increasingly important, as nowadays, a number of species are included in salads, including the cultivated mushroom (*Agaricus bisporus*) and the penny bun bolete (*Boletus edulis*).

In the case of wild edible mushrooms, a number are known to cause stomach upsets when eaten raw. At worst, the resulting symptoms may involve nausea, abdominal pain and cramp, vomiting and diarrhoea, with a full recovery after a few hours. These mushrooms include the honey fungus (*Armillaria mellea.*), the red-stalked bolete (*Boletus luridiformis*) and the related *Boletus luridus*, the peppery brittle gills (*Russula*) and milk caps (*Lactarius*), the blewits (*Lepista*), the roman shield (*Entoloma clypeatum*), the chicken of the woods (*Laetiporus sulphureus*) and the morels (*Morchella*).

There is a further group of wild mushrooms which should

not be eaten in the raw state: those containing toxins which produce the haemolytic syndrome. The toxins, which still remain largely unknown, break down the red corpuscles in the blood stream, and their depletion can result in anaemia and, in extreme cases, lead to kidney blockage. The latter is likely to result only when a considerable amount of the offending mushroom is eaten. The symptoms, usually causing pallor, manifest themselves about four hours or so following ingestion. The toxins causing haemolysis are thermolabile, that is to say they are inactivated and destroyed by heat: hence, if the mushroom is thoroughly cooked, and the water discarded after parboiling, it may be safely eaten.

Blood cell-damaging mushrooms belong to the genus *Amanita*, although there are some suggestions that morels and certain cup fungi might also fall into this category. Avoid experimenting with any species of *Amanita* unless you are absolutely sure of your identification. The species involved may be divided into two groups: **the blusher** (*Amanita rubescens*, page 182) and its relatives; and the **grisette** (*A. vaginata* page 184).

The blusher

Amanita rubescens

Reddish brown cap with small, greyish scales; reddening flesh; stem with ring but no volva

Gills white, closely crowded together, eventually getting pinkish spots

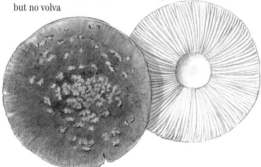

Cap convex, then flattened, reddish brown but can vary from pale cream to yellowish brown or even dark vinaceous brown, bearing small light grey patches

Stem cylindrical, expanding towards the base, but never showing a cup-like volva or rim, with a persistent, hanging, membranous, white or sometimes yellowish ring

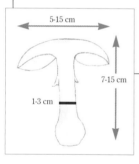

5-15 cm

7-15 cm

1-3 cm

Spore print

Flesh white, reddening on exposure

Frequency very common

Spore deposit white

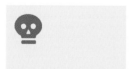

One of Europe's commonest mushrooms, the blusher occurs in deciduous and coniferous woodland. In fact, it can be an edible mushroom (page 102), but only if thoroughly cooked – indeed it is commonly eaten in Eastern Europe. An identifying feature is discolouration of the white flesh when the fruitbody is broken open, slowly changing to pink or reddish brown, especially around holes made by insect larvae. However, the blusher is very variable, both in colour and form, and is confused with several species, especially the poisonous panther (page 214 and opposite). If eaten raw and in large quantities, it causes, about four hours later, stomach upset and abdominal cramps. If untreated, severe anaemia can result.

182

Habitat
In both deciduous and coniferous woodland

LOOKALIKES

The panther
Amanita pantherina The panther may be distinguished from the blusher by the white flesh which does not redden, the small, white warty scales on the cap surface, the striated margin of the cap, and the stem base which has a series of irregular rings of scales. Contains ibotenic acid, a toxin that affects the central nervous system. *See page 214.*

The grisette

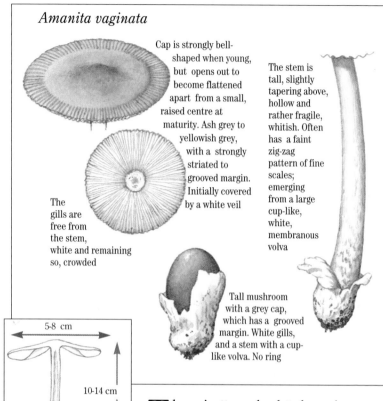

Amanita vaginata

Cap is strongly bell-shaped when young, but opens out to become flattened apart from a small, raised centre at maturity. Ash grey to yellowish grey, with a strongly striated to grooved margin. Initially covered by a white veil

The stem is tall, slightly tapering above, hollow and rather fragile, whitish. Often has a faint zig-zag pattern of fine scales; emerging from a large cup-like, white, membranous volva

The gills are free from the stem, white and remaining so, crowded

Tall mushroom with a grey cap, which has a grooved margin. White gills, and a stem with a cup-like volva. No ring

5-8 cm

10-14 cm

Spore print

Flesh thin, white and brittle, with a mild smell

Spore deposit white

Frequency very common

The grisette and related species are a distinctive group of red cell-damaging fungi. The absence of a ring on the stem for many years placed them in a separate genus, *Amanitopsis*, but the differences in variations in the development of the fruit-body are slight, and the distinction is rarely accepted today. Although edible when cooked, the grisette is best avoided unless you are an expert, as it can be easily confused with other *Amanita* species which have lost their ring.

Eating

✗ ✗ **DO NOT EAT RAW**

Only edible after cooking – poisonous when raw. Frequently eaten in central and eastern Europe, although they are of moderate quality and usually mixed with other species.

184

Habitat
Under leafy places where there is plenty of leaf litter, often by the sides of paths

LOOKALIKES

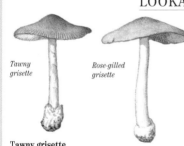

Tawny grisette

Rose-gilled grisette

Paddy straw mushroom
Volvariella volvacea. An edible species widely cultivated and eaten throughout Southeast Asia, and nearly always found in Chinese cuisine. It grows off sawdust or decaying straw. The conical cap grows to about 5 cm across, coloured yellowish brown, and appears streaky, the gills are white then pink, and the solid stem is white.

Rose-gilled grisette
Volvariella gloiocephala. Also known as *Volvariella speciosa*. Although closely resembling the grisettes, this species belongs to a completely different family, the *Pluteaceae*. It is tall, with a sticky, pale grey cap, and the stem emerges from a large, white sack-like volva. However, the gills are pink, and produce pink rather than white spores.

Tawny grisette
Amanita fulva. Often more common than the grisette, but very similar apart from a tawny orange cap deepening to dark reddish brown at the centre. Until recent years only these two grisettes were recognized but several other species have now been described in Europe, to form a fairly large group.

Hallucinogenic mushrooms and alcohol-related poisoning

Liberty caps

The best known and most common mushrooms of this type are the **liberty caps** (*Psilocybe semilanceata*, page 188) and related *Psilocybe* species.

Historically, the use of magic mushrooms goes back to religious and ritualistic activity in Central America, by the Ancient Mexican Aztecs, with documentation dating back 2000 years. The importance played by these mushrooms in early societies may be reflected by the abundance of Mayan stone-mushroom relics. Since the 1950s, use of the magic mushroom has spread throughout North America, Europe and Australia to the point where drug abuse legislation now exists to cope with the use of these mushrooms.

In Central America, the Teonanacatl (*Psilocybe mexicana*) is most widely used, whilst in much of North America and Europe, this is replaced by the liberty cap. In North America, the most popular mushroom for this purpose is the **golden tops** (*Psilocybe cubensis*, page 189), partly because it forms a more fleshy fruitbody and also because it is relatively easily cultivated in 'kitchen-laboratories'. One of the main dangers with these mushrooms is that they are small, brown, and generally lack distinctive features. It is therefore very likely that other, similar yet deadly poisonous species may be gathered in error.

Golden top

These mushrooms principally contain psilocybin, which is a tryptamine acting on the central nervous system. Psilocin and baeocystin are also frequently present, both precursors of psilocybin. Psilocybin was first isolated, from *Psilocybe mexicana*, in 1958. Its symptoms closely parallel those caused by LSD (lysergic acid diethylamide). Initially, often within 20-60 minutes after eating, there is anxiety and possibly aggressive behaviour, followed by drowsiness or nausea. Visual and auditory distortions follow, then attacks of panic and possibly fear of death. After two to three hours, visual distortions may increase, perhaps with brilliant colours and geometrical patterns. The physical symptoms include pupil dilation, rapid breathing, lowering of body temperature, and rise in blood pressure. Normally these effects last from eight to 12 hours, and normality return after 24 hours. However, flashbacks can occur and these may be repeated for up to four months. Deaths have occurred, mainly involving children, although the main hazard is likely to be a tendency towards dangerous behaviour.

The **common ink cap** (*Coprinus atramentarius*, page 194) might be considered a good, edible mushroom, as is the equally common, **shaggy ink cap** (*Coprinus comatus*, page 106). Unfortunately, it contains a compound, called coprine which is a condensation product of glutamine and cyclopropanine. When the mushroom is eaten together with an alcoholic drink, extremely unpleasant symptoms result. Such a reaction will occur even if alcohol is consumed up to 24 hours earlier. Remember that alcohol can occur in a hidden form in many food products, including salad dressings. So, avoid all ink caps, with the exception of the shaggy ink cap.

Common ink cap

Coprine acts to arrest alcohol metabolism, allowing the build-up of the toxic acetaldehyde. For many years, such cases seemed similar to that of the 'antabuse' (disulfiram) reaction, used as a deterrent drug in the remedial treatment of alcoholism. Coprine is now known to have a quite different formulation. The onset of symptoms is very early, possibly within ten minutes, and includes an unpleasant metallic taste, extensive blushing of the face and neck, rapid heart rate, chest pains and severe headaches. These may last up to two hours but will be repeated at any time over the next five days if alcohol is drunk again. There are several other species of ink caps reported to produce similar symptoms, and most are closely allied to the common ink cap.

There are reports of similar reactions caused by the **club-footed funnel cap** (*Clitocybe clavipes*, page 196).

Club-footed funnel caps

Liberty cap

Psilocybe semilanceata

Tall, small mushroom; narrow sticky cap
with projection; purplish black gills

Gills adnexed,
purplish black
with a white
edge, crowded

Cap strongly conical with central
projection, not expanding, pale brown,
sticky and smooth, with an often greyish
and incurved margin

Stem tall and
slender, paler than
cap, smooth

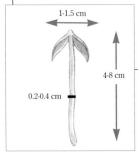

1-1.5 cm

4-8 cm

0.2-0.4 cm

Spore print

Flesh thin, firm, white

Frequency very common

Spore deposit purplish black

This species is the commonest cause of fungal poisoning because of its use as a hallucinogen. People mix it up with more dangerous mushrooms: many small, brown fungi grow with liberty caps, and are easily confused.

This is, in fact, one of the 'magic mushrooms', and in Britain possession is an offence. Great numbers can occur in fields, especially early in the season after rain. The name derives from its similarity with the hat adopted at the time of the French Revolution.

Symptoms start after 15 minutes to two hours, and include headaches, confusion, muscular weakness and mental disturbance. Recovery is generally within six to ten hours but cases of 'flashbacks' are often recorded.

Habitat
In grassland,
including lawns

LOOKALIKES

Golden tops
Psilocybe cubensis Cap
3-6 cm across, bell-
shaped or convex, pale
with yellowish brown
centre, staining bluish;
gills adnate, purplish black;
stem 5-15 x 0.2-0.4 cm, white
soon staining blue at base, with
Golden tops
a white, membranous ring at
top; on dung. Tropical
American but evidence of
illegal importation into
Europe, and easily grown in
'kitchen laboratories'.

Fairy ring champignon
Marasmius oreades Very common in
grassland. Cap light brown, gills whitish and
spaced; always appear in groups. *See page 72.*

Marginate pixy cap
Galerina marginata
Small brown
fruitbodies, tufted on
dead conifer wood; cap
convex to flattened, with
brown gills, and a fibrous ring
on stem. Has been mistaken
for liberty cap, but deadly
poisonous. *See page 172.*

*Marginate
pixy cap*

Brown hay cap
Panaeolina foenisecii
Extremely common on lawns
and in short grass from early
summer onwards. Cap bell-
shaped, dark grey drying to clay brown, gills
dark, mottled; stem relatively short. Most
frequently mistaken for the liberty cap. *See
page 191.*

Girdled mottle gill

Panaeolus subbalteatus

Small tufts; cap and stem dark blackish brown drying paler; gills mottled, on composted flower-beds

Cap strongly convex to conical, then expanding with a raised centre, dark reddish-brown to almost black when moist, drying to pale reddish brown, slightly ridged or cracked at the centre, otherwise smooth

Gills adnate, reddish brown becoming mottled and finally black, with a white edge, crowded

Stem cylindrical, reddish brown or darker when moist, drying paler, often slightly bluish at the base or bruising blue, longitudinally striated

Spore print

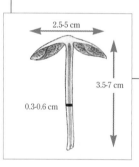

2.5-5 cm

3.5-7 cm

0.3-0.6 cm

Flesh thin, greyish, without a distinctive smell

Frequency occasional to fairly common

Spore deposit black

The girdled mottle gill usually appears in groups, sometimes in large numbers, and can often be found on composted flower-beds. There are several related and very similar species. Like several of the mottle gills (*Panaeolus* species), some bluish discoloration may occur at the stem base or when the stems are bruised. Species in this group that bruise blue in this way should be avoided because they have been shown to contain psilocin and psilocybin, which are capable of psychotropic poisoning.

Symptoms start early, within two hours, and include confusion and muscular weakness, together with mental disturbance. Recovery is after a few hours, but some suffer repeated panic attacks.

Habitat
On enriched or
manured,
disturbed soil

LOOKALIKES

Brown hay cap
Panaeolina foenisecii Cap 1-2 cm across,
bell-shaped to convex, greyish brown,
paling from centre; gills adnate, dark
brown, mottled; stem 3-5 x 0.2-0.3 cm,
paler than cap; spore deposit blackish
brown; June to October, very common in
short grass and lawns; also known as
'mower's mushroom'.

Orange scale head

Gymnopilus junonius

Fruitbodies large and clustered at base of trees; cap and stem orange; large rings on stem; gills and spore deposit rusty brown

Cap strongly convex, finally expanding, fleshy, golden brown to orange-brown, with tiny, flat, brown scales

Gills adnate, yellowish brown finally rusty brown, crowded

Stem thick, slightly paler than cap, with a brown, membranous ring towards the top

6-12 cm

6-15 cm

1-3 cm

Spore print

Flesh thick, firm, yellowish, with a very bitter taste

Frequency common

Spore deposit rusty brown

The orange scale head is also known as the orange Pholiota and *Pholiota spectabilis*.

It can cause hallucination, owing to its psilocybin content. In Japan, the species has acquired the popular name of 'big laughing gym' because it can produce fits of uncontrolled laughter.

The very bitter taste should deter most people from experimenting with the orange scale head – and it should be avoided, not least because it can be easily confused with the many deadly poisonous web caps (*Cortinarius* species).

Besides hallucination and mood changes, symptoms include problems with balance. Recovery is after six to ten hours.

192

Habitat
Forms large
clusters on old
trunks, stumps
and buried roots
of leafy trees

LOOKALIKES

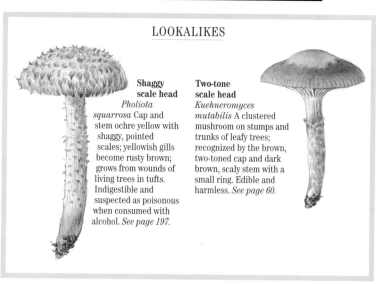

Shaggy scale head
Pholiota squarrosa Cap and stem ochre yellow with shaggy, pointed scales; yellowish gills become rusty brown; grows from wounds of living trees in tufts. Indigestible and suspected as poisonous when consumed with alcohol. *See page 197.*

Two-tone scale head
Kuehneromyces mutabilis A clustered mushroom on stumps and trunks of leafy trees; recognized by the brown, two-toned cap and dark brown, scaly stem with a small ring. Edible and harmless. *See page 60.*

Common ink cap

Coprinus atramentarius

Large, tufted ink cap, bell-shaped grey cap;
liquefying gills; ring-zone at stem base

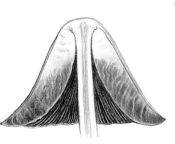

Cap rounded to bell-shaped,
only partially expanding, grey,
smooth, striated, with a few
tiny, brown scales at the centre

Gills free, densely
crowded, white
becoming grey-black and
finally liquefying

Stem cylindrical,
white, brittle,
hollow, with a ring-
zone near the base

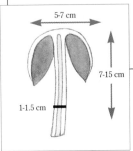

5-7 cm

7-15 cm

1-1.5 cm

Spore print

Flesh thin, soft, watery-white,
with little smell

Frequency common

Spore deposit black

Often mistaken for the edible shaggy ink cap and almost as common, this fungus is found in tufts of about ten or so fruitbodies, usually around the roots of trees, often in urban locations. Like all ink caps, the gills dissolve into a black inky liquid and dissolve the cap. Similar, closely related species include *Coprinus acuminatus*, with a central, pointed knob, and *Coprinus romagnesianus*, with rusty brown scales at the apex.

It causes unpleasant, sometimes even violent reactions within ten minutes when consumed with alcohol (see page 187) or if alcohol has been drunk recently – or indeed if eaten with food that has been cooked with alcohol. Reactions can recur up to 48 hours after eating.

Habitat
Forms tufts at
bases of trees
and stumps
throughout the
year

LOOKALIKES

Shaggy ink cap
Coprinus comatus Tall cylindrical, pure
white cap with tiers of white, curly scales,
liquefying gills. Commonly found in grassland
and parkland, sometimes in very large
numbers. Edible and excellent. *See page 106.*

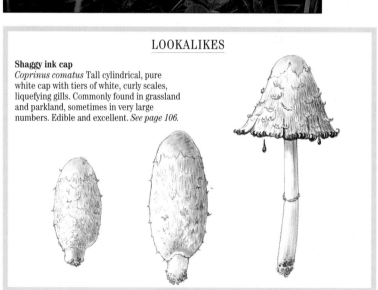

195

Club-footed funnel cap

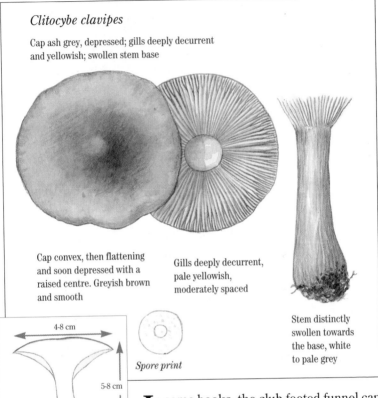

Clitocybe clavipes

Cap ash grey, depressed; gills deeply decurrent and yellowish; swollen stem base

Cap convex, then flattening and soon depressed with a raised centre. Greyish brown and smooth

Gills deeply decurrent, pale yellowish, moderately spaced

Spore print

Stem distinctly swollen towards the base, white to pale grey

4-8 cm

5-8 cm

0.5-1 cm

Flesh thick, white, with a smell of bitter almonds and a sweetish taste

Frequency occasional to frequent

Spore deposit white

In some books, the club-footed funnel cap is described as an edible species, but a number of cases are recorded of the mushroom causing unpleasant symptoms if eaten with alcohol. However, the presence of coprine (see page 187) has so far not been isolated in this fungus, and the cause of the symptoms is not entirely clear. Even so, it is sensible to avoid drinking alcohol before, during, or for some time after a meal that features this particular mushroom.

It resembles the small, clouded agaric (*Lepista nebularis*, see opposite), but is distinguished by the strangely swollen stem base and widely spaced gills.

Symptoms include early onset of vomiting, and skin rashes.

Habitat
Amongst litter
in leafy and
conifer woods

LOOKALIKES

**Clouded
agaric**
Lepista nebularis
Common, forming
large troops
amongst leaf litter
in woodlands. Cap
ash grey with
yellowish tints,
gills creamy-white
and crowded;
stem stout. Easily
confused with the
club-footed funnel cap.
Inedible, often indigestible.

**Shaggy scale
head**
Pholiota squarrosa
Reported to cause alcohol-
related reactions although
this may be due to general
stomach upsets being
enhanced by alcohol
consumption. *See page 47.*

Sweat-inducing mushrooms

Common white fibre caps

Red-staining fibre cap

Cream clot

The compound muscarine causes increased perspiration, salivation and weeping, and muscarine poisoning usually arises from mistaken identification. Examples of this include: the **common white fibre cap** (*Inocybe geophylla*, page 200), mistaken for liberty caps; the **red-staining fibre cap** (*Inocybe patouillardii*, page 202) mistaken for the St. George's mushroom; the **cream clot** (*Clitocybe dealbata,* page 204) mistaken for the fairy ring champignon and the **copper trumpet** (*Omphalotus olearius,* page 206), mistaken for the chanterelle.

The term muscarine is derived from the mushroom *Amanita muscaria*, or the **fly agaric** (*Amanita muscaria,* page 212), from which it was originally extracted, although only in very small amounts. The fly agaric was the first fungus to have had an active compound extracted. Until fairly recently, the compound was thought to be the cause of all mushroom poisonings. Fly agaric also contains the psychoactive compounds, ibotenic acid and muscazone (see page 210), which produce intoxicating effects.

Fly agarics

Muscarine also occurs in a large number of mushrooms, especially those belonging to the funnel caps (*Clitocybe* species) and the fibre heads (*Inocybe* species) known as the sweat-inducing mushrooms. In the case of the fibre heads, there are more than one hundred species, of which about 40 are known to contain muscarine. In the funnel caps, at least 13 species, generally the white species, contain the substance. Eating them results in an early onset of symptoms, from 15 minutes to two hours later. This combination is not found in any other kind of mushroom poisoning and has become known as the PSL-syndrome. In severe cases, additional digestive symptoms appear, including stomach cramps, nausea, vomiting and diarrhoea, together with a lowering of blood pressure and blurred vision. Poisoning has caused a few deaths, usually the result of cardiac or respiratory failure. The effects of the poisoning can be reversed by giving atropine.

Common white fibre cap

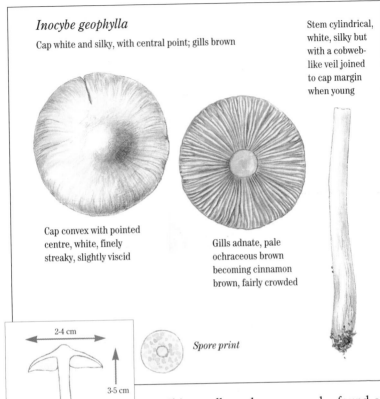

Inocybe geophylla

Cap white and silky, with central point; gills brown

Stem cylindrical, white, silky but with a cobweb-like veil joined to cap margin when young

Cap convex with pointed centre, white, finely streaky, slightly viscid

Gills adnate, pale ochraceous brown becoming cinnamon brown, fairly crowded

2-4 cm

3-5 cm

0.3-0.5 cm

Spore print

Flesh firm, white, with an earthy smell

Frequency common

Spore deposit clay brown

This small mushroom may be found on the ground in open woodland, sometimes growing in very large numbers. The combination of its uniform white colour and brown gills should make it easy to identify. Even so, many people have suffered muscarine poisoning from this species because they think that it is the hallucinogenic liberty cap (page 188).

The lilac fibre cap (opposite), although a very different colour, is merely a variety of the common white fibre cap and also contains muscarine. The two varieties often grow together in large numbers.

Symptoms appear 15 to 30 minutes after eating and feature sweating, weeping, vomiting and diarrhoea. Seek medical help.

Habitat
Leafy woods

LOOKALIKES

Lilac fibre cap
Inocybe geophylla var *lilacina* Similar to the common white fibre cap apart from the lilac cap and stem, occasionally with a yellowish cap centre.

Liberty cap
Psilocybe semilanceata A cream to pale brown mushroom, with blackish gills and spore deposit, growing in open grassland, containing psychotropic compounds. *See page 188.*

Red-staining fibre cap

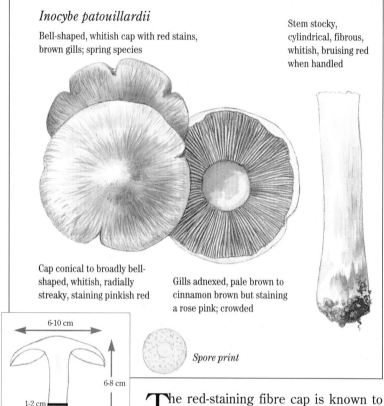

Inocybe patouillardii

Bell-shaped, whitish cap with red stains, brown gills; spring species

Stem stocky, cylindrical, fibrous, whitish, bruising red when handled

Cap conical to broadly bell-shaped, whitish, radially streaky, staining pinkish red

Gills adnexed, pale brown to cinnamon brown but staining a rose pink; crowded

6-10 cm

6-8 cm

1-2 cm

Spore print

Flesh white, reddening when exposed to air, with an unpleasant, fetid smell

Frequency occasional

Spore deposit clay brown

The red-staining fibre cap is known to contain a high concentration of muscarine and has caused serious illness or even death.

The most dangerous of the fibre caps, it occurs early in the spring months, and for this reason is sometimes collected alongside, and confused with, the edible St. George's mushroom (page 74). The rounded, unopened white caps also lead to confusion with the true mushrooms (*Agaricus* species). Be alert for the red staining of all parts, and the brown gills and spore deposit.

Typical muscarine-poisoning symptoms are sweating, weeping and salivating, together with severe stomach upset.

Habitat
Amongst grass
on chalky soil,
at woodland
edges

LOOKALIKES

St. George's mushroom
Calocybe gambosa Robust
mushroom, with whitish convex
to expanding cap, crowded white
gills, and a strong floury smell,
growing in grassland during the
spring. Edible. *See page 74.*

Cream clot

Clitocybe dealbata

Depressed, whitish cap; short decurrent, crowded gills, amongst grass

Gills short decurrent, white, very crowded

Cap convex, flattened to depressed, whitish to cream or with pale pinkish tints, smooth, with a down-curved margin

Stem short cylindrical, same colour as cap, fibrous

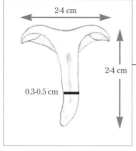

2-4 cm

2-4 cm

0.3-0.5 cm

Spore print

Flesh thin but firm, white, with a mealy smell

Frequency fairly common

Spore deposit white

The cream clot appears slightly later in the season than the fairy ring champignon (page 72), but is often confused with it. Found in similar situations, and both forming fairy rings, they can even grow together with rings intermingled. Take the greatest of care: the cream clot contains large quantities of muscarine and can cause serious illness. Always check for decurrent gill attachment.

A larger species, *Clitocybe cerussata*, with a white, depressed cap, 6 to 8 cm across, and a floury smell, appears in conifer woods and is equally poisonous. Symptoms usually start 15 to 30 minutes after eating, and include sweating and weeping, with cramps, vomiting and blurred vision. Seek medical help.

Habitat
Amongst short grass, lawns and pastures, often as a fairy ring

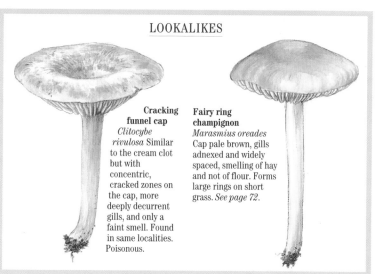

LOOKALIKES

Cracking funnel cap
Clitocybe rivulosa Similar to the cream clot but with concentric, cracked zones on the cap, more deeply decurrent gills, and only a faint smell. Found in same localities. Poisonous.

Fairy ring champignon
Marasmius oreades Cap pale brown, gills adnexed and widely spaced, smelling of hay and not of flour. Forms large rings on short grass. *See page 72.*

205

Copper trumpet

Omphalotus olearius

Bright orange, funnel-shaped cap; deep
decurrent orange gills, tufted at bases of trees

Gills deeply decurrent,
yellowish orange, crowded

Cap depressed to funnel-
shaped, saffron yellow to
bright orange, smooth

Spore print

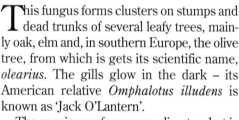

Stem cylindrical,
tapering towards the
base, saffron yellow
or darker below

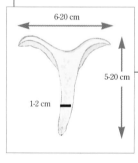

6-20 cm

5-20 cm

1-2 cm

Flesh thin, firm, yellowish

Frequency occasional

Spore deposit cream

This fungus forms clusters on stumps and
dead trunks of several leafy trees, mainly oak, elm and, in southern Europe, the olive
tree, from which is gets its scientific name,
olearius. The gills glow in the dark – its
American relative *Omphalotus illudens* is
known as 'Jack O'Lantern'.

The species prefers warm climates, but is
occasionally found in southern England. It
would probably never be eaten except that its
yellowish orange colours lead to confusion
with the much prized chanterelles (page 24).
Most poisonings occur in the Mediterranean
countries, usually by tourists unfamiliar with
the fungus.

Symptoms include headaches, sweating,
nausea and vomiting.

Habitat
Tufted, on stumps and base of trees, in warmer regions of central and southern Europe

LOOKALIKES

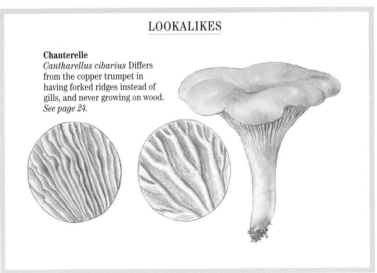

Chanterelle
Cantharellus cibarius Differs from the copper trumpet in having forked ridges instead of gills, and never growing on wood. *See page 24.*

Lilac bonnet cap

Mycena pura

Lilac or pinkish cap; lilac, spaced gills; tall stem

Cap bell-shaped to flattened,
varying from whitish to bluish
lilac or pinkish, smooth

Gills adnate, pale
lilac, well spaced

Stem delicate,
cylindrical,
blue-lilac to
greyish, smooth

Spore print

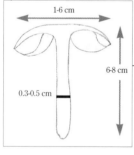

1-6 cm

6-8 cm

0.3-0.5 cm

Flesh thin but firm, watery
white, with a smell of radish

Frequency common

Spore deposit white

This is one of the larger bonnet caps
(*Mycena* species), commonly found,
though usually growing on its own.

The species is variable in colour, ranging
from lilac or pinkish to almost white. It is
distributed widely in almost every country
of the world, and contains small amounts of
the poison muscarine. Avoid confusion with
the amethyst deceiver (page 59).

The bonnet caps are a large group, run-
ning to about 150 species in Britain and
Europe. Nearly all of them are harmless –
and not worth eating.

Symptoms appear soon after eating and
include sweating, weeping and stomach
upsets.

Habitat
Amongst leaf
litter in
woodlands

LOOKALIKES

Common navel cap
Omphalina ericetorum Cap 1-2
cm across, funnel-shaped, pale
yellowish brown with darker
furrows; gills decurrent, cream;
stem 2-3 x 0.5-0.7 cm, short,
yellowish brown; on peat in
damp situations. Harmless.

Ibotenic acid poisoning

Fly agarics

The panther

Isoxazole compounds, such as ibotenic acid and muscazone, cause psychotropic poisoning, which often resembles that of alcoholic intoxication. Two common mushrooms, the **fly Agaric** (*Amanita muscaria*, page 212) and **the Panther** (*Amanita pantherina*, page 214), are known to contain such compounds. Although they are both species of *Amanita*, the poisoning is quite distinct from that caused by the cyclopeptides found in the death cap and allied species, but can be fatal. Similarly, the effects on the central nervous system differ from those caused by the magic mushrooms.

There is a long history and folklore dealing with the uses of the fly agaric as a narcotic drug. Even today, it is widely misused as a so-called recreational drug, so that cases of poisoning usually result from eating it voluntarily, rather than from misidentification. The mushroom gets its name from the traditional use as an insecticide in central and eastern Europe. The fruitbody is cut into small pieces and placed in a saucer of milk, which attracts and kills houseflies.

It has been treated as a sacred mushroom in many parts of the world, and there are even suggestions that the 'soma' plant of the ancient Indian book, *Rig Veda*, refers to the fly agaric. The frenzies generated by the Viking tribes, the Beserks, are thought to have resulted from eating fly agaric. Probably the most documented use of the mushroom is that of the Shaman priests of Siberia, with references dating back to at least the 17th Century. It played a central and revered role in Shamanistic practices and its use was restricted to sacred occasions. Ingestion could take the form of either rolling pieces of the mushroom into a ball and swallowing whole, use in a soup, soaked in bilberry juice, or concentrated in urine and re-ingested. The effects depend on dosage, the place of collection and the psychological expectations of the consumer. The results range from feelings of increased strength and vitality to a state of tranquillity. The initial effect is often one of gastric upsets, including nausea, vomiting and diarrhoea, but this is followed by increased physical activity and then both auditory and visual hallucinations. Finally, stupor and sleep take over, followed by a severe hangover.

Although the poisoning can be serious, including coma, fatalities are very rare. Trading of the fly agaric became a profitable business in Siberia and continued until vodka was introduced by the Russians as an alternative intoxicant. The hallucinations can include the perception of persons and objects out of scale (macro- and microscopical) and this was taken up by Lewis Carroll in *Alice's Adventures in Wonderland*. It may also explain the origins of Santa Claus, as the Shaman priests would normally enter the primitive, half-buried houses of the population through a hole in the roof, otherwise the chimney, and the red coat with a white trim may reflect the fly agaric.

Fly agaric

Amanita muscaria

Flat cap scarlet red, with concentric red scales; free white gills; stem with ring and volval scales on stem base

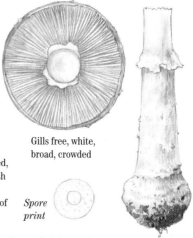

Cap at first rounded then strongly convex, expanding and finally depressed, scarlet red, shiny, often fading yellowish towards the edge; covered with large, snow white, irregular, cottony patches of the veil, which are easily detached

Gills free, white, broad, crowded

Spore print

Stem cylindrical with a swollen base, white, finely scaly, with a large, hanging, membranous ring towards the top and fragmenting remains of the volva over the base, reduced to small, white scales

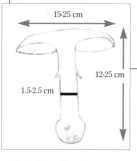

15-25 cm

12-25 cm

1.5-2.5 cm

Flesh white, firm, fleshy with a weak taste and smell

Frequency very common

Spore deposit white

The most easily recognized of all common mushrooms, fly agaric is large, with a scarlet red cap and white scales. It is the subject of many an illustration, especially in children's books, and is unlikely to be confused, except possibly in Mediterranean areas, with Caesar's mushroom (page 98). Containing ibotenic acid and muscazone, fly agaric can be used as a hallucinogen (see page 210); but the amounts present are only small and need to be concentrated to have a significant effect. It also contains the sweat-inducing poison, muscarine. Poisonings mostly occur from recreational misuse. A mixture of symptoms start within 30 minutes of eating: sweating, weeping, abdominal pains and mental disturbance.

Habitat
On the ground
in small groups
in both conifer
and leafy woods,
especially birch

LOOKALIKES

Caesar's mushroom
Amanita caesarea Differs in
having yellow gills, ring and stem,
a large, white, sack-like volva,
and grows under oak or chestnut.
See page 98.

The panther

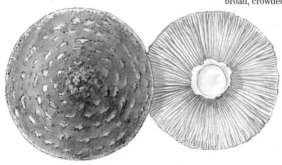
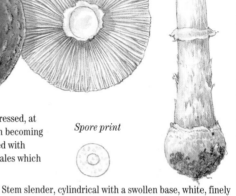

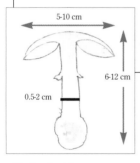

The panther can cause serious poisoning, generally more severe than that of the fly agaric (*Amanita muscaria,* page 212).

The active ingredient is ibotenic acid, although the amount in a specimen does depend on the time and place of collection. A significant number of poisoning cases occur, both in Europe and North America, usually as a result of confusion with the blusher (*Amanita rubescens,* page 182) which, after cooking, is considered an edible species. In fact, it is one of the commonest causes of non-fatal mushroom poisoning.

The symptoms generally begin 30 to 60 minutes after eating, but are sometimes delayed for six hours. There is nervous excitation, possibly also delirium and coma.

Habitat
On the ground
in both leafy
and pine woods

LOOKALIKES

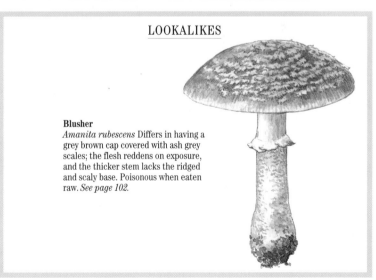

Blusher
Amanita rubescens Differs in having a
grey brown cap covered with ash grey
scales; the flesh reddens on exposure,
and the thicker stem lacks the ridged
and scaly base. Poisonous when eaten
raw. *See page 102.*

Digestive system irritants

Yellow stainers

The largest group of 'poisonous mushrooms' may be placed together under the heading digestive system irritants, in other words they cause stomach upsets. These are responsible for the majority of all fungal poisonings, perhaps as high as 40 per cent of all recorded cases. However, as the recovery period is usually fairly rapid, it is certain that many more cases go unrecorded. In Europe, the most common culprits are the **yellow stainer** (*Agaricus xanthoderma*, page 218), the **livid pink gill** (*Entoloma sinuatum*, page 220) and **the sickener** (*Russula emetica*, page 230). A number of species are apparently edible and enjoyable in certain situations but will cause problems in others. The **honey fungus** (*Armillaria mellea*, page 44) is a good edible mushroom when young, fresh fruitbodies are used, but older fruitbodies will almost always cause gastric upsets.

Another problem lies with the **brown roll rim** (*Paxillus involutus*, page 233). The precise mechanism of poisoning remains unclear. In eastern Europe, it has long been used as a source of food, apparently without any ill effects, apart from stomach upsets when eaten raw. However, in recent years, several cases of severe poisoning, including deaths, have been recorded, although no toxin has been identified. There is some evidence that repeated consumption may have a cumulative effect over many years. The Paxillus-syndrome, as its symptoms have become known, includes icy

Sickeners

extremities, stomach cramps, sweating, loss of consciousness, and haemolytic anaemia leading to kidney failure. There is a general view that this is an immuno-haemolytic allergy, which only affects some individuals.

Many mushrooms act as irritants of the wall linings of the alimentary canal, and this may result from eating them either in the raw state, cooked, or in large quantities. The causes are generally non-specific, and the causes, often proteins, remain unidentified. These

Livid pink gills

mushrooms are characterized by showing only a short latent period, ranging from 15 minutes to two hours, rarely longer, before onset of symptoms. These are largely gastro-intestinal, with vomiting, abdominal pains, stomach cramps, and diarrhoea. Recovery is usually within a few hours, exceptionally, one to two days, and no special treatment is generally required. The effects are likely to lead to dehydration, so plenty of water should be drunk. In rare cases, the symptoms may be more severe and deaths have been recorded. Mushrooms that irritate the digestive system should, therefore, never be underestimated.

A number of poisonings follow after eating raw mushrooms, and these could increase as the use of 'salad fungi' in the home becomes more popular. Often, these mushrooms contain thermo-labile compounds, which are destroyed by heat and thereby become harmless when cooked. In other cases, any toxins may be removed by first parboiling the mushrooms and then discarding the water. Such is the case with many of the brittle gills (*Russula*), milk caps (*Lactarius*) and blewits (*Lepista*).

The mushrooms which form this group are varied, ranging from the gill-fungi to the boletes, the coral fungi, and the puff-ball families. In the following pages are the principal examples encountered in Europe and North America.

Yellow stainer

Agaricus xanthoderma

Large and fleshy, white fruitbody, staining bright yellow;
stem base flesh chrome yellow; large ring; smell of phenol

Cap strongly convex with a
flattened top then expanding,
pure white, dry, often
cracking, bruising chrome
yellow when rubbed

Gills free, pale pink
finally turning chocolate
brown, crowded

Spore print

Stem cylindrical with slightly swollen
base, white, bruising yellow or brownish,
bearing a large, hanging, membranous
ring which has a scaly underside

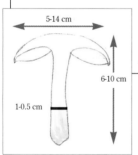

5-14 cm

6-10 cm

1-0.5 cm

Flesh thick and white and
immediately changes to bright
chrome yellow at the stem
base, with a distinctive strong
smell of carbolic or ink

Frequency very common early
in season

Spore deposit purplish brown

This is one of the few true mushrooms
(*Agaricus* species) which is dangerous
and to be avoided, and one of the commonest causes of mushroom poisoning. It resembles cultivated mushrooms (page 37) and
field mushrooms (page 36), with pale pinkish gills darkening to chocolate brown or
purplish black; and it is especially easy to
confuse with the horse mushroom (page
38). In both, the surfaces bruise yellow when
rubbed; the acid test is to cut open the stem
base – if it stains chrome yellow, you have a
yellow stainer. Unless 100 per cent sure of
identification, avoid all mushrooms that stain
yellow when rubbed.

Symptoms begin 15 minutes to two hours
after eating, usually causing stomach upsets.

Habitat
Often as clusters in leaf litter, especially in gardens and under hedgerows

LOOKALIKES

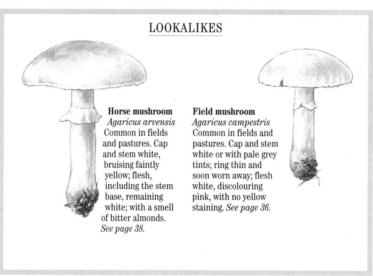

Horse mushroom
Agaricus arvensis
Common in fields and pastures. Cap and stem white, bruising faintly yellow; flesh, including the stem base, remaining white; with a smell of bitter almonds. *See page 38.*

Field mushroom
Agaricus campestris
Common in fields and pastures. Cap and stem white or with pale grey tints; ring thin and soon worn away; flesh white, discolouring pink, with no yellow staining. *See page 36.*

Livid pink gill

Entoloma sinuatum

Flesh cap and stem pale yellowish to greyish brown; gills becoming pink; no veils; early season species

Cap convex with a raised centre, pale, yellowish brown to greyish brown, smooth, with inrolled margin

Gills sinuate, pale grey to yellowish becoming pink, crowded

Stem stocky, pale grey and fibrous

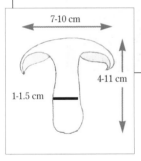

7-10 cm

4-11 cm

1-1.5 cm

Spore print

Flesh thick, pale brown, with faint smell of cucumber or of meal

Frequency occasional

Spore deposit pink

There are many pink gills (*Entoloma* species), all distinguished by pink spores visible in the spore deposit and on gills of older fruitbodies. Some are edible: these generally occur in the spring, but need to be identified by an expert.

Many more species are poisonous, and probably the most dangerous of these is the livid pink gill. It is the largest of the pink gills and, when young, can be confused with St George's mushroom, (page 74). Fleshy mushrooms with pink gills and spore deposits should be avoided.

Symptoms usually begin 20 minutes to two hours after eating and can be intense, with severe stomach cramps. Liver damage can occur, and deaths have been recorded.

Habitat
Scattered in open places in leafy woods

LOOKALIKES

Rosy pink gill
Entoloma rhodopolium Cap 5-12 cm across, greyish to yellowish brown, radially streaky; stem elongated, up to 12 cm, whitish, no smell; autumn, in leafy woods. *Entoloma nidorosum* is similar but more slender and has a nitrous smell.

Silky pink gill
Entoloma sericeum Cap 3-6 cm across, dark brown drying out to pale grey brown, silky shiny; stem similarly coloured; smell very mealy; common on lawns and grassland, in autumn.

221

Tiger knight cap

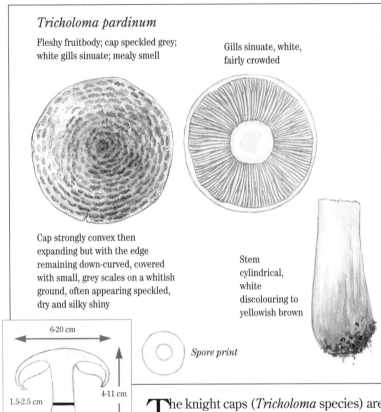

Tricholoma pardinum

Fleshy fruitbody; cap speckled grey; white gills sinuate; mealy smell

Gills sinuate, white, fairly crowded

Cap strongly convex then expanding but with the edge remaining down-curved, covered with small, grey scales on a whitish ground, often appearing speckled, dry and silky shiny

Stem cylindrical, white discolouring to yellowish brown

6-20 cm

1.5-2.5 cm

4-11 cm

Spore print

Flesh white, with a mealy smell

Frequency occasional

Spore deposit white

The knight caps (*Tricholoma* species) are generally large and fleshy, with white or pale gills and a stem with no ring. A few are considered edible but the genus is best avoided, particularly those with grey, scaly caps or reddish brown caps. The tiger knight cap is the one to be most wary of – it has caused many poisonings in central Europe, especially in Germany and Switzerland, usually the result of it being confused with the clouded agaric (page 197). However, it is not found in Britain.

Eating it produces violent symptoms of vomiting, diarrhoea and extreme thirst. This can last for several days, but then recovery is rapid.

Habitat
In groups in mixed woods throughout Europe but not in Britain

LOOKALIKES

Soap-scented knight cap
Tricholoma saponaceum
Cap 4-10 cm across, greyish, yellowish to olive green, often cracking; widely spaced, sinuate gills; white stem; in troops under trees, recognized by soapy, carbolic smell.

Soap-scented knight cap

Poisonous. Can cause similar, less severe symptoms to tiger knight cap.

Silky grey knight cap
Tricholoma portentosum
Cap 5-12 cm across, grey with dark radial fibres, sticky when moist; gills white tinted grey; stem white; under pine or oak. Good edible species but requires accurate identification.

Silky grey knight cap

Grey knight cap
Tricholoma terreum In mixed woods, but prefers conifers. Cap grey to almost black, felty, fibrous; gills and stem are whitish. Edible when young but best avoided as it is easily confused with other grey knight caps.

Golden wax cap

Hygrocybe chlorophana

Cap and stem lemon yellow;
cap slimy; fruitbody brittle

Cap strongly convex soon
flattened, orange to lemon
yellow, slimy and striated
when moist, shiny when dry

Gills adnexed, at first
whitish soon lemon
yellow, broad, widely
spaced

Stem cylindrical or
flattened with
central groove, with
tapering base, same
colour as cap or paler

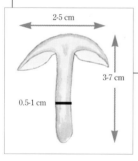

2-5 cm

3-7 cm

0.5-1 cm

Spore print

Flesh thin, pale yellow,
without any significant smell

Frequency fairly common

Spore deposit white

Although this mushroom is typically a shade of yellow, it can be very changeable as the cap, gills or stem can become much paler, or acquire greenish yellow or even scarlet tints.

The wax caps (*Hygrocybe* species) are brightly coloured, grassland mushrooms, with shiny caps and stems and an attractive waxy appearance. They have been known to cause stomach upsets, but the identity of the species involved has often been imprecise. The golden wax cap is definitely a culprit – so it is best to avoid any fungus with a waxy appearance. Symptoms start soon after eating and may include nausea and vomiting. Recovery is rapid.

Habitat
In groups in grassland, lawns and dunes

LOOKALIKES

Large scarlet hood

Large scarlet hood
Hygrocybe punicea
The largest wax cap.
Cap 4-12 cm across,
conical then
expanding with a
raised centre,
scarlet red, fading to
yellowish; gills
adnexed, yellow to
orange-red; stem 5-15 x 1-2 cm, cylindrical,
orange-red, yellow towards the base.
Poisonous.

Witch's hat
Hygrocybe conica Entire fruitbody blackens
when handled. Cap 2-8 cm across, conical,
yellow-orange to reddish orange, silky
streaky, blackening with age; gills adnexed,
white to sulphur yellow, blackening; stem 3-
11 x 0.5-1.5 cm, cylindrical, sulphur yellow to
orange, blackening. Common everywhere,
including woods, roadsides and lawns.
Poisonous.

Liquorice milk cap

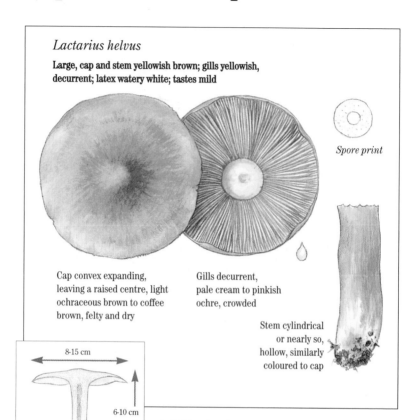

Lactarius helvus

Large, cap and stem yellowish brown; gills yellowish, decurrent; latex watery white; tastes mild

Spore print

Cap convex expanding, leaving a raised centre, light ochraceous brown to coffee brown, felty and dry

Gills decurrent, pale cream to pinkish ochre, crowded

Stem cylindrical or nearly so, hollow, similarly coloured to cap

8-15 cm

6-10 cm

2-3 cm

Flesh thick, whitish, brittle, releasing a watery-white, mild tasting latex; and a distinct smell of chicory or liquorice

Frequency fairly common

Spore deposit whitish with faint pink tinge

This is the only species of milk cap known to be truly poisonous, even though it tastes mild. It is however used dried, as a spice, in small quantities.

Those species of milk cap that taste pungent cause gastric disorders and should be avoided although some milk caps are eaten in east and north-east Europe, but only after first boiling and discarding the water. In fact, it is generally agreed that all milk caps are best avoided, with the exception of those which produce a red to orange latex, such as the saffron milk cap (page 92) and its relatives.

Symptoms include nausea, vomiting and diarrhoea about 30 minutes after being eaten.

Habitat
In conifer
woods (pine)
and under birch

LOOKALIKES

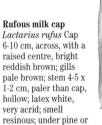

Rufous milk cap
Lactarius rufus Cap
6-10 cm, across, with a
raised centre, bright
reddish brown; gills
pale brown; stem 4-5 x
1-2 cm, paler than cap,
hollow; latex white,
very acrid; smell
resinous; under pine or
birch. Inedible, owing to hot taste, but fried
and used for seasoning in eastern Europe.

Ugly milk cap
Lactarius necator
Cap 10-15 cm across,
dirty olive brown
with a blackish
centre, and inrolled
edge; gills white,
spotted brown; stem
2-3 x 1-1.5 in (5-8 x 2-
3 cm), paler; latex
white drying greenish grey; under birch.
Inedible, owing to hot taste, except in
eastern Europe where eaten after parboiling
or preserving in salt. *See page 95.*

Peppery milk cap

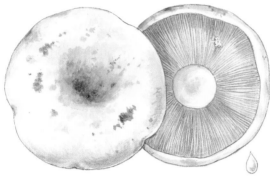

Lactarius piperatus

White, robust and stocky fruitbody; very crowded, narrow gills; white acrid latex

Spore print

Cap convex soon depressed and irregular with wavy margin; white, with pale brown patches

Gills curved decurrent, creamy white, narrow and very crowded

Stem stocky, tapering below, solid but brittle, white

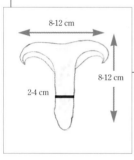

8-12 cm

8-12 cm

2-4 cm

Flesh thick and fleshy, brittle, producing a copious white latex which dries pale greenish yellow, with a very hot taste

Frequency common

Spore deposit white

The hot, acrid tasting milk caps, including the peppery milk cap, are generally unpalatable to western tastes and can cause gastric upsets. But they are frequently eaten in Scandinavian countries, usually after parboiling, discarding the water, then frying.

The woolly milk cap (*Lactarius torminosus*), with its pinkish, woolly cap, marked paler and darker in concentric zones, also has a very acrid taste, yet is regarded as a delicacy in parts of northern Europe, again after parboiling. The pungent milk caps can be tested by tasting a tiny fragment of the raw mushroom. After a few minutes, a hot burning sensation is experienced at the back of the throat.

Habitat
Under leafy trees, especially beech and hazel

LOOKALIKES

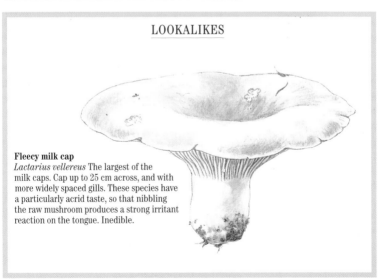

Fleecy milk cap
Lactarius vellereus The largest of the milk caps. Cap up to 25 cm across, and with more widely spaced gills. These species have a particularly acrid taste, so that nibbling the raw mushroom produces a strong irritant reaction on the tongue. Inedible.

The sickener

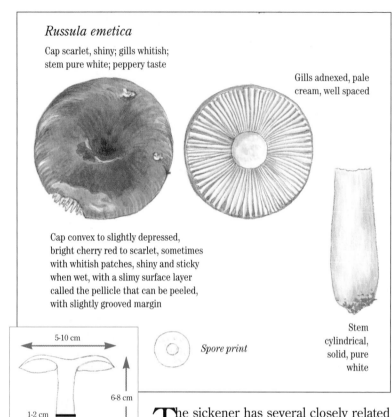

Russula emetica

Cap scarlet, shiny; gills whitish;
stem pure white; peppery taste

Gills adnexed, pale
cream, well spaced

Cap convex to slightly depressed,
bright cherry red to scarlet, sometimes
with whitish patches, shiny and sticky
when wet, with a slimy surface layer
called the pellicle that can be peeled,
with slightly grooved margin

Stem
cylindrical,
solid, pure
white

5-10 cm

Spore print

6-8 cm

1-2 cm

Flesh thick, white, crumbly,
with a slightly fruity smell

Frequency common

Spore deposit white

The sickener has several closely related
varieties and species. The beechwood
sickener (*Russula mairei*) is similar, but
smaller, firmer and grows under beech. The
brittle gills are similar, too, but have a squat
appearance; their stems are thick and rarely
longer than the cap width; often, the cap is
brightly coloured and the flesh crumbly.
Identifying individual species can be hard.
Red pigments in mushrooms tend to be both
soluble and destroyed by sunlight, so very
pale forms are common. Edible species have
a mild taste – try a tiny piece on the tip of the
tongue, and if it is hot and peppery, spit it out.

Symptoms include abdominal pains, vomiting and diarrhoea, whether the fungus is
eaten raw or cooked.

Habitat
Under pine or birch trees, preferring wet situations

LOOKALIKES

Stinking brittle gill
Russula foetens Cap 10-15 cm across, strongly convex, dull yellowish brown, slimy, with grooved margin; gills cream; stem 8-13 x 3-4 cm, whitish, hollow; very peppery with a smell of rancid oil; in woodlands. Inedible.

Poison pie

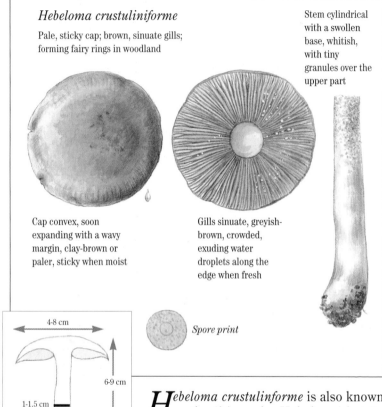

Hebeloma crustuliniforme

Pale, sticky cap; brown, sinuate gills; forming fairy rings in woodland

Stem cylindrical with a swollen base, whitish, with tiny granules over the upper part

Cap convex, soon expanding with a wavy margin, clay-brown or paler, sticky when moist

Gills sinuate, greyish-brown, crowded, exuding water droplets along the edge when fresh

4-8 cm

6-9 cm

1-1.5 cm

Spore print

Flesh firm, white, with a bitter taste and strong smell of radish

Frequency common

Spore deposit clay-brown

*H*ebeloma crustulinforme is also known as the 'fairy cake Hebeloma' but its very bitter taste does not support this description. The apparently weeping gills are a distinctive feature.

All Hebeloma species resemble pale knight caps (*Tricholoma* species) and have brown gills and a brown spore deposit. Most occur in very large numbers, often forming large fairy rings. The pine hebeloma (*Hebeloma mesophaeum*) is smaller, with a date brown cap and ring-zone on stem, whilst the clay hebeloma (*Hebeloma sinapizans*) has a large, pink-brown cap and smell of radish.

They have a bitter taste and should be avoided as they cause gastric upsets.

Habitat
In leafy woods
and heathland,
sometimes
under conifers
and forming
rings

LOOKALIKES

Brown roll rim
Paxillus involutus Very common on heathlands and in mixed woods, usually under birch trees. Cap 5-20 cm across, depressed with an inrolled margin, olive brown, sticky when wet; gills decurrent, cream to reddish brown, spotted red-brown, crowded, soft and easily detached; stem 4-7 x 1-1.5 cm, short, pale brown becoming spotted with reddish brown. Poisonous.

Sulphur tuft
Hypholoma fasciculare Common, forming tufts on dead stumps. Cap 2-4 cm across, sulphur yellow; gills greenish becoming purplish brown, crowded; stem sulphur yellow, with dark ring-zone, spore deposit blackish brown. Poisonous, with bitter taste; can cause liver damage.

Blood-red web cap
Dermocybe sanguinea
Dermocybe are a small group of mushrooms closely related to the web caps *(Cortinarius* species). They have a reddish to yellowish brown, dry, smooth cap and stem. The blood red web cap has cap, stem and gills that are uniformly blood red. Poisonous, containing anthraquinones, which produce laxative and possibly other gastric symptoms, and should be avoided.

Brown roll rim

Blood-red web cap

Devil's bolete

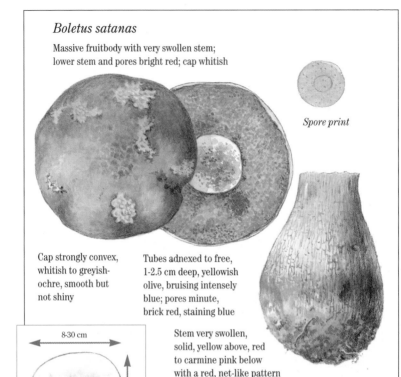

Boletus satanas

Massive fruitbody with very swollen stem; lower stem and pores bright red; cap whitish

Spore print

Cap strongly convex, whitish to greyish-ochre, smooth but not shiny

Tubes adnexed to free, 1-2.5 cm deep, yellowish olive, bruising intensely blue; pores minute, brick red, staining blue

Stem very swollen, solid, yellow above, red to carmine pink below with a red, net-like pattern

8-30 cm

5-14 cm   7-12 cm

Flesh very thick, cream to yellow but slowly discolouring blue, with a mild taste but an unpleasant smell of rotting meat

Frequency rare to occasional

Spore deposit brown

Most boletes are edible, but it is wise to avoid any bolete with red pigment in case it is muddled with the Devil's bolete, which causes disturbances to the digestive system. No toxins have been isolated, however. Its strong reddish colouring and unpleasant smell contribute to its reputation.

This is a distinctive species, one of the largest boletes, commonest in warm regions, growing on chalky soil under beeches. In Britain, it is listed as an endangered species because of its comparative rarity.

Raw or undercooked fruitbodies can cause stomach upsets and indigestion, but the species is eaten in central Europe.

Habitat
On chalky soil,
under beech,
sometimes oak;
more common
in southern
Europe; in
Britain confined
to southern
England

LOOKALIKES

Peppery bolete
Chalciporus piperatus
Cap 3-6 cm across,
convex, dull brown,
sticky when moist;
pores small,
cinnamon brown;
stem 4-10 x 1-2 cm,
cylindrical and
reddish brown but tapering with a bright
yellow base; on sandy soil, under birch and
pine. Poisonous, with strong peppery taste.

Bitter bolete
*Tylopilus
felleus* Cap
4-15 cm
across,
brown, dry and
cracking; pores
minute, white to pale
pink; stem 7-12 x 2-3
cm, swollen at base,
pale brown, with a
brown network; spore
deposit clay pink; on
sandy soil, under
beech and oak. Easily
confused with the penny
bun bolete (*page 120*) which has a white
network on the stem. Intensely bitter taste
that ruins any dish.

Common earthball

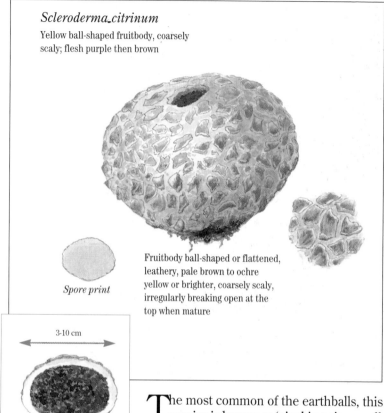

Scleroderma citrinum

Yellow ball-shaped fruitbody, coarsely
scaly; flesh purple then brown

Spore print

Fruitbody ball-shaped or flattened,
leathery, pale brown to ochre
yellow or brighter, coarsely scaly,
irregularly breaking open at the
top when mature

3-10 cm

Flesh (gleba) purplish black
and marbled when young, firm,
fleshy but becoming brown
and powdery as the spores
mature

Frequency very common

Spore deposit fuscous brown

The most common of the earthballs, this
species is known as 'pigskin poison puffball' in the USA. When broken open, the
young fruitbodies reveal a purplish black,
mottled flesh which superficially resembles
that of a black truffle (see page 150). These
are frequently mistaken for the underground
truffles and have sometimes even been used
to adulterate commercially sold truffles. Old
fruitbodies are more distinctive, as they
break open to reveal dense masses of brown,
powdery spores. There are six closely related earthball species in Europe. These need
not be confused with the true puffballs
(*Lycoperdon*), which are all edible and good
when young. When eaten raw, earthballs can
cause abdominal pains and cramps.

Habitat
Commonly found on soil in sandy heaths and woodland, especially under beech, oak and birch

LOOKALIKES

Scaly earthball
Scleroderma verrucosum Fruitbody 3-6 cm across, ball-shaped but usually with a stem-like base, reddish brown to ochre, with many small scales becoming smooth; flesh purplish black then brown and powdery, in leafy woods and heathland. Poisonous.

Summer truffle
Tuber aestivum Up to 9 cm across, blackish brown with polygonal warts; flesh whitish to olive brown, marbled; buried in chalky soil under beech. Edible. *See page 151.*

Allergies and contamination

An allergy is an abnormal reaction to an otherwise harmless substance. Some people are particularly sensitive to the cultivated mushroom (page 37), and similar allergic sensitivity to wild mushrooms is just as common. Such hypersensitivity is thought to affect about 15 per cent of the population. Eating the mushroom causes antibodies to be formed which react specifically to the substance in question. Generally, the symptoms are gastro-intestinal disturbances, together with headaches, although a 'nettle-rash' on the skin can also result.

Cultivated mushroom

The reaction might be due to the polysaccharide chitin, the substance which forms most of the mushroom fruitbody. Chitin, on the other hand, is completely indigestible and symptoms may result from simply eating too great a volume causing blockage in the alimentary canal. In other cases, allergies may result from the inhalation of clouds of spores which are released from the actively growing mushrooms. This is often apparent in the mushroom-growing industry, resulting in a syndrome called 'mushroom worker's lung', causing asthma, conjunctivitis and rhinitis, with perhaps joint pains and headaches. The oyster mushroom (page 132) has, in the past, proved a particular problem. The spores may originate either from the mushrooms themselves or from the many contaminating mould fungi which are always present.

Clouded funnel cap

There are suggestions that certain wild mushrooms contain a substance called hydrocyanic acid, which may produce allergies. Species often mentioned here belong to the genus blewits, and include the wood blewit (page 78) and the clouded funnel cap (page 197), but this still needs to be confirmed. Finally, there may be an antibiotic reaction, whereby the bacteria normally present in the gut are attacked, and the giant funnel cap (*Leucopaxillus giganteus*) has been identified as a possible villain.

Poisoning can be caused by contamination of mushrooms through herbicides, pesticides, road dust and traffic fumes that may contain lead or mercury. Never collect by the roadside. Wild mushrooms readily absorb heavy metals and are also susceptible to contamination from radioactive fallout, such as from the Chernobyl disaster.

Oyster mushrooms

Cooking with mushrooms

If you have bought this book, the chances are that you are keen not only to learn about edible mushrooms, but to eat them, too. In the main part of the book, we give brief hints on how to cook each type of wild edible mushroom described, but here we offer what we hope is a useful collection of mushroom recipes, both homely and sophisticated, chosen to help you enjoy the best qualities of edible fungi.

Having read the book, you may by now be longing to cook with mushrooms, but, not having any wild ones to hand, be quite willing to make do with shop-bought (cultivated) ones, instead. With this in mind, most of the recipes have been chosen for their suitability for either. A few of the recipes require specific mushrooms, such as the Italian recipes for pasta and rice which call for boletes (penny bun bolete in English, *cep* in French, *porcini* in Italian), as well as the recipes for stuffed mushrooms.

Above right
Common morel

Left Penny bun
bolete

Preparing mushrooms

On the whole, mushrooms should be handled as little as possible before cooking. Remove any blemishes, wipe them over with a damp cloth, trim the stalks if necessary. Slice, or cut into pieces if they are large. Morels need a little more work: cut them in half and wash.

Drying mushrooms

Wild mushrooms are very easy to dry, and several species are excellent candidates for use in recipes, in particular ceps (boletes), which retain a remarkable amount of flavour and always add distinction to dishes in which they are used.

Mushrooms should be allowed to dry in an even temperature as quickly as possible. In warm climes they can be simply left out in the open air, but in cooler countries, they should be spread out on newspaper (boletes should be thinly sliced), and left to dry in an airing cupboard, or on a rack on top of an Aga or oil-fired stove. They should become shrivelled and brittle, without first going mouldy, in anything from 24 hours to a few days. When they are quite dry, pack them into airtight jars or brown paper bags. To reconstitute, soak them in warm water, then drain and gently squeeze them dry. If the recipe requires stock, the soaking water can often be used to give extra flavour.

A general-purpose method for cooking wild mushrooms

Most mushrooms have an affinity with butter, onion and garlic, lemon juice, parsley and cream. Trim and wipe clean your mushrooms. In a frying pan, soften some finely chopped onion and garlic in butter, then turn into an ovenproof dish, adding the mushrooms, salt and freshly ground black pepper, a squeeze or two of lemon juice and some chopped parsley. Cook in a moderate oven for an average of 15 minutes, depending on the type of mushroom. Stir in some cream if desired. Nothing could be more delicious than a mixture of mushrooms cooked in this way and served on rounds of hot buttered toast.

Remember, when using wild mushrooms, that their cooking times will vary according to the type and age of the mushrooms, and that they tend to exude more liquid than cultivated mushrooms, some of which may have to be poured off. Also, be more generous with stated quantities than with cultivated mushrooms.

Starters, light dishes and accompaniments

Mushroom soup with mustard

SERVES 4

3 oz/75 g butter
1 onion, peeled and finely
chopped
12 oz/350 g mushrooms,
sliced or roughly chopped if
necessary
1 pt/570 ml chicken stock
4 tbs dry sherry
1 tbs Dijon mustard
small bunch thyme, chopped
5 fl oz/150 ml single cream
salt and freshly ground black
pepper
small bunch parsley, chopped
(optional)

Served piping hot, this soup makes a good starter for a dinner party. The chicken stock should be homemade or ready prepared, but not made from a stock cube.

Melt the butter in a saucepan, add the onion and fry gently for a few minutes until the onion is soft, but not brown. Add the mushrooms and cook for a further 5 minutes until they are soft and the juices have begun to run. In a separate saucepan, heat the chicken stock until simmering, then pour onto the mushrooms, adding the sherry. Bring to the boil, and simmer for about 10 minutes. Stir in the mustard and thyme, and season with salt and pepper to taste. Allow the soup to cool a little, then liquidise. Reheat gently, adding the cream and adjusting the seasoning. Serve in warm bowls, with a sprinkling of chopped parsley in each, and plenty of crusty bread.

Quick mushroom soup

Here is another recipe for mushroom soup, quick and simple to make, perfect for a family meal.

Melt the butter in a saucepan, and cook the garlic and mushrooms for about 5 minutes, until the juices run. Add the stock, the bread and seasoning. Simmer for about 20 minutes. Allow to cool a little, then liquidize, adding the parsley. Taste, adjust seasoning and serve in warm bowls, adding, if you wish, a swirl of cream to each.

SERVES 4

1 oz/25 g butter
1 clove garlic, peeled and finely chopped
8-12 oz/225 – 350 g mushrooms, sliced or
roughly chopped if necessary
1 pt/570 ml chicken stock
2 medium slices brown bread
salt and freshly ground black pepper
small bunch parsley, chopped
a little cream (optional)

Stuffed mushrooms

Serves 4

4 large flat mushrooms
2 oz/ 50 g butter
1 onion, peeled and
finely chopped
8 rashers streaky bacon,
chopped
1 tbs parsley, chopped
1 tbs mixed fresh herbs such as
thyme, rosemary, sage,
chopped
2 tbs fresh white breadcrumbs
salt and freshly ground black
pepper

There are few better ways of eating mushrooms than this. Parasol mushrooms or horse mushrooms are ideal, or you can use flat mushrooms from the shops. Serve as a light lunch dish with salad, or as a starter.

Preheat the oven to gas mark 4, 350 degrees F, 180 degrees C.

Remove any stalks from the mushrooms and chop them. Melt 1 oz/ 25 g of the butter and fry the onion and bacon until soft and beginning to brown. Add the mushroom stalks and stir in the parsley, the other mixed herbs and the breadcrumbs. Cook for 5 minutes over a gentle heat. Season to taste. Divide the mixture equally amongst the mushrooms, put a dot of butter on each one, place on a baking sheet and bake in the oven for 15-20 minutes.

Mushrooms stuffed with cream cheese

These savoury mushrooms can be served as part of a selection of canapés, or as a starter, allowing about four mushrooms per person. You can use field mushrooms or cultivated mushrooms. As a starter, serve them on individual plates, on a bed of mixed salad leaves, sprinkled with a little vinaigrette.

SERVES 4

16 open cup mushrooms
1 oz/25 g butter
7 oz/ 200 g cream cheese
4 oz/ 110 g cheddar cheese, grated
2 tbs parsley, finely chopped
grated rind and juice of ½ lemon
salt and pepper

Carefully remove any stalks from the mushrooms and discard. Melt the butter in a frying pan, and briefly fry the mushrooms, cap side down, to lightly brown them.

Mix together the cream cheese, 2 oz/50 g of the cheddar cheese and the parsley. Add enough lemon rind and juice to taste, and salt and pepper. Mix thoroughly until smooth, then with a teaspoon fill each mushroom with the mixture. Sprinkle the remaining 2 oz/50 g cheddar cheese over the mushrooms and place under a hot grill for 5 minutes, or until golden brown.

Spinach, bacon and mushroom salad

A favourite way of using mushrooms suitable for eating raw, but beware of those mushrooms which cannot be eaten raw (see page 217). In this recipe, the salad is given a touch of sophistication by the addition of mixed leaves, ready prepared in bags from the supermarket, walnuts and a vinaigrette flavoured with walnut oil.

Fry the bacon rashers in a little oil or bacon fat until crisp. Drain on kitchen paper. In a large salad bowl, mix together the spinach leaves and the salad leaves. Halve the avocado, remove the stone, scoop out the flesh and cut into slices. Add the chopped bacon, the mushrooms, and the avocado slices to the bowl.

To make the vinaigrette, whisk together the oils and vinegar, adding more walnut oil or balsamic vinegar to taste. Stir in the mustard, and season with salt and black pepper. Shake or whisk well, and pour onto the salad. Toss, and sprinkle over the walnuts.

SERVES 4

8 rashers streaky bacon
4 oz/110 g young spinach leaves, washed
4 oz/110 g mixed salad leaves
1 large or 2 small ripe avocado
8 oz/225 g mushrooms, sliced
2 oz/50 g walnut halves
For the vinaigrette:
4 tbs olive oil
2 tbs walnut oil
2 tbs balsamic vinegar
1 tsp Dijon mustard
salt and freshly ground black pepper

Spaghetti with mushrooms and prawns

Penny bun bolete

An elegant way of serving ceps (penny bun boletes). Other edible boletes can be substituted. The recipe makes an excellent starter, but you could increase the quantities and serve it as a main course. Parmesan cheese can be substituted for pecorino.

SERVES 4

14 oz/400 g spaghetti or spaghettini
4 tbs extra virgin olive oil
1 clove garlic, finely chopped
2 spring onions, finely chopped,
including the green part
1 dried red chilli, finely chopped
8 oz/225 g ceps, wiped clean and sliced
8 oz/225 g prawns
5 fl oz/150 ml white wine
salt and freshly ground black pepper
2-3 tsp pesto sauce
2 tbs pecorino cheese, grated
1 tbs parsley, chopped

Cook the spaghetti until *al dente* in abundant boiling salted water. Meanwhile, heat the oil and briefly sauté the garlic, spring onion and chilli, then add the sliced mushrooms and continue to cook over a medium to low heat for a few minutes. Add the prawns, then stir in the wine, allowing the liquid to bubble up; cook gently for a few minutes more. Season to taste with salt and pepper. Just before serving, stir in the pesto. Drain the pasta, add the sauce, toss, and serve on individual plates, garnished with pecorino and parsley.

Brioches filled with mushrooms

SERVES 4

8 brioches
2 oz/50 g butter
2 tbs flour
1/2 pint/275 ml milk
4 oz/110 g mushrooms,
chopped very small
2 slices ham, chopped very small
2 oz/50 g Gruyère cheese, grated
1 tsp fresh rosemary, chopped,
or dried
salt and freshly grated black pepper

The sweet French bread, brioche, makes a perfect vehicle for stuffing with a variety of fillings, in this case, mushrooms, ham and cheese. Brioches are available from good bakeries and most large supermarkets. In France, the dish would be served as an entrée, but it also makes a light main course. You could also use the mixture to fill vol-au-vent cases.

In a saucepan, melt 1 oz /25 g butter, and stir in the flour. Cook for a minute or two without allowing to colour, then remove the pan from the heat and pour on the milk. Return to the heat, and cook, stirring, until the sauce is thick and smooth. Season.

In a small frying pan, melt the remaining butter and cook the mushrooms over gentle heat until soft. Season with a little salt and pepper, then stir in to the béchamel sauce along with the ham. Stir in the cheese and the rosemary, and adjust the seasoning.

Preheat the oven to gas mark 2, 300 F, 150 C. Remove the tops from the brioches, and scoop out the insides without piercing them. Heat them in the oven. Fill them with the mixture and serve immediately.

Main dishes

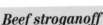

Beef stroganoff

A classic recipe for beef fillet. Simply assemble the ingredients in advance, and cook at the last minute. Serve with buttered noodles and a green salad.

In a frying pan, heat the butter and cook the shallots until soft. Stir in the paprika, cook for about half a minute, and then add the mushrooms, turning up the heat so that they cook rapidly. With the heat still high, add the vinegar. When it has almost evaporated (about a minute), add the brandy, allow to bubble for about half a minute, then add the chicken stock, and allow the liquid to cook until reduced to about half. Season with salt and pepper, turn down the heat, and stir in the sour cream. Keep warm over a very low heat. In a separate frying pan, heat the olive oil until very hot, then add the strips of beef. Cook over high heat for about 3 minutes. With a slotted spoon, remove the beef from the pan and stir it into the sauce. Reheat, and serve immediately.

SERVES 4

1¼ lb/600 g beef fillet, cut into thin strips
1 oz/25 g unsalted butter
3-4 shallots, peeled and finely chopped
1 tbs paprika
6 oz/175 g mushrooms, sliced thinly
2 tbs white wine vinegar
4 tbs brandy
7 fl oz/200 ml chicken stock
7 fl oz/200 ml sour cream
3 tbs olive oil
salt and freshly ground black pepper

Braised pork with mushrooms

An easily assembled pot roast (using cubes of meat, rather than a whole piece) A mixture of wild mushrooms is best; if using cultivated ones, include, if possible, 2 oz /50 g of dried ceps to deepen the flavour. In this case, use the strained soaking water instead of chicken stock (which should be homemade or ready prepared, but not from a cube).

Orange birch rough stalk

SERVES 4

1½ lb/700 g diced pork
5 tbs olive oil
1 onion, finely chopped
1 large or 2 small cloves of garlic,
finely chopped
8 oz/225 g mushrooms, sliced or
roughly chopped if necessary
2 tbs white wine vinegar
5 fl oz/150 ml white wine
5 fl oz/150 ml chicken stock
25 juniper berries, crushed
1 bayleaf
a few sprigs marjoram
salt and freshly ground black pepper

Preheat the oven to gas mark 3, 325 degrees F, 170 degrees C. Heat the oil in an oven-proof casserole, and fry the onion and garlic until soft but not brown. Turn up the heat, add the pork, in batches if necessary, and fry until brown. Remove with a slotted spoon. Now reduce the heat, add the mushrooms, and cook until soft – about 5 minutes. Turn the heat to high, add the vinegar and allow to bubble up for a minute. Add the wine, stock and strained water (if using), the juniper berries, bayleaf, marjoram and a generous seasoning of salt and black pepper. Cook for 1½ hours or until the meat is tender.

Stir-fried chicken with mushrooms

SERVES 4

1 lb/450 g boneless chicken thighs or
breast, cut into strips
3 tbs groundnut oil
1 clove garlic, finely chopped
1 tsp ginger, finely chopped
2 tbs spring onion, including the green
part, chopped
6 oz/175 g mushrooms, thinly sliced
2 tbs dry sherry
2 tbs dark soy sauce
2 tbs chicken stock or water
½ tsp sugar
coriander leaves to garnish

For the marinade:

2 tsp light soy sauce
2 tsp dry sherry
1 tsp sesame oil
2 tsp cornflour

Here is an Oriental recipe in which you can use either Chinese shitake mushrooms, or you can substitute European mushrooms such as button, field, horse, jelly fungi or oyster mushrooms. For preference use a wok, although a frying pan will do.

Half an hour in advance, mix together the marinade ingredients in a bowl. Add the chicken, coating it well, and leave aside.
Heat 1 tbs of the oil in the wok or frying pan, then add the garlic, ginger and spring onion. Cook for a minute or two, then add the chicken and stir fry over a brisk heat until browned. Remove the chicken and keep warm. Add another 2 tablespoons of oil, and quickly fry the mushrooms. Return the chicken to the pan, and stir in the sherry, soy sauce, stock or water and sugar. Continue to cook gently for another 10 minutes. Serve garnished with sprigs of coriander.

Mushroom tart

A perfect dish for a lunch party, served with warm French or ciabatta bread and a simple green salad. If you are using cultivated mushrooms instead of wild, it would be a good idea to include some dried ceps as well (2 oz/50 g dried ceps and 6 oz/150 g fresh cultivated mushrooms).

SERVES 4

8 oz/225 g shortcrust pastry, ready prepared or homemade
4 eggs
7 fl oz/200 ml crème fraîche
grated nutmeg
salt and freshly ground black pepper
handful of basil leaves
2 oz/50 g butter
1 onion, finely chopped
1 clove garlic, finely chopped
8-10 oz/225-275 g mushrooms, sliced

Line a 10 inch flan dish with the pastry. Prick with a fork, then put it in the fridge for 30 minutes.

Preheat the oven to gas mark 6, 400 degrees F, 200 degrees C. Line the pastry with greaseproof paper, cover with dried beans and bake blind in the oven for 10 minutes.

Crack the eggs into a mixing bowl, beat them with a fork, then whisk in the crème fraîche, mixing until smooth. Add a couple of good pinches of grated nutmeg, salt and plenty of black pepper. Roughly tear the basil leaves with your hands (don't use a knife as this bruises them), and add to the mixture.

In a frying pan, melt the butter, add the onion and garlic, and cook for a minute or two until soft. Add the mushrooms and continue to cook very gently for about 10 minutes. Season, then remove from the heat. Spread the mushrooms over the pastry, pour over the egg and crème fraîche mixture, and cook in the oven for 20 to 30 minutes until firm to the touch and just turning golden brown.

Mushroom and egg pie

A simple stand-by for times when you have only minimal ingredients on hand.

SERVES 4

6 oz/175 g shortcrust pastry, ready prepared or homemade
1 lb/450 g mushrooms, sliced or roughly chopped if necessary
4 hard boiled eggs, sliced
5 fl oz/150 ml single cream
salt and pepper

Preheat the oven to gas mark 6, 400 degrees F, 200 degrees C.

Put the mushrooms, eggs, cream and seasoning into a small oven-proof pie dish and cover with the pastry. Bake for about thirty minutes, until the pastry has browned.

Mushroom and spinach soufflé

Cooking times for soufflés can vary, depending on your oven. The time given here is a guideline only. Avoid the temptation to keep checking the soufflé as it cooks. When you think it might be ready, prod it with a long metal skewer: it should come away clean, and the soufflé should be well risen and firm but still soft in the centre.

Serves 4

6 oz/175 g young spinach
leaves, stalks removed
2 oz/50 g butter
1 large or 2 small cloves
garlic, finely chopped
6 oz/175 g mushrooms,
sliced or chopped small
2 tbs flour
7 fl oz/200 ml milk
6 eggs, separated
salt and freshly ground
black pepper
nutmeg
1 tbs Parmesan cheese,
grated

Preheat the oven to gas mark 5, 375 degrees F, 190 degrees C.

Wash the spinach, and put directly from the water into a saucepan. Cook gently, without adding extra water, until the leaves are just wilted. Drain, cool slightly, squeeze out any excess water and chop finely.

Melt 1 oz/25 g of the butter in a saucepan. Add the garlic and cook briefly. Add the mushrooms and continue to cook gently until soft and the juices have started to run. Turn the heat to high and continue cooking rapidly until the juices have almost evaporated, stirring constantly. Remove the mushrooms to a bowl, leaving behind any liquid. Mix the spinach with the mushrooms. Season with salt and pepper.

In a saucepan, melt the remaining 1 oz/25 g of butter, then stir in the flour. Cook, stirring, over a low heat for 2 minutes without allowing the flour to colour. Remove from the heat, pour on the milk, then return to the heat and cook, stirring, until the sauce is thick and smooth. Remove the pan from the heat, cool slighly, then add the egg yolks, incorporating them one at a time. Season with salt, pepper and grated nutmeg. Turn the spinach and mushroom mixture into the white sauce, and amalgamate evenly. Adjust the seasoning.

Whisk the egg whites until they make soft peaks. Reheat the spinach and mushroom mixture, then remove from the heat. Stir in one tablespoon of the egg whites, then fold in the rest. Turn into a buttered soufflé dish, sprinkle the top with Parmesan, and cook for approximately 30 minutes until risen and golden. Serve immediately.

Mushroom risotto

SERVES 4

6 oz/17 g Arborio or similar
Italian risotto rice
2 oz/50 g dried ceps
3 tbs olive oil
2 oz/50 g butter
1 large or 2 small cloves
garlic, finely chopped
8 oz/225 g mushrooms,
sliced or roughly chopped
7 fl oz/200 ml dry white wine
½ pt/275 ml good chicken
stock
salt and freshly ground
black pepper
2 tbs Parmesan cheese,
grated

An authentic Italian risotto, creamy and fragrant, and superb when cooked with wild mushrooms, particularly ceps. Even if you are using wild mushrooms, rather than cultivated ones, you should include some dried ceps so that you can make use of their soaking water when adding the liquid to the rice. Like a soufflé, the risotto should be eaten as soon as it is ready.

About half an hour before you make the risotto, soak the dried ceps in 14 fl oz/400 ml hot water. In a large frying pan, heat the oil and 1 oz/25 g butter, and add the garlic and the fresh mushrooms. Strain the ceps, reserving the water, squeeze them dry, and add to the pan. Cook, stirring, until the mushroom juices begin to run, for about 5 minutes. Add the rice, stirring, until the grains become somewhat transparent, about a minute or two, then add the white wine, allowing it to bubble up. When the wine has almost disappeared, start adding the stock and the reserved mushroom water, in alternate ladlefuls. As one ladleful becomes absorbed, add another one, until the rice is just tender, and very creamy. Season with salt and black pepper, stir in the cheese, and serve immediately.

Spaghetti with mushroom sauce

As with risotto, this is a dish which is perfectly suited to ceps. In smaller quantities, it could equally well be served as a starter. Hand round freshly grated Parmesan.

Cook the spaghetti until *al dente* in plenty of boiling salted water.

Meanwhile, melt the butter in a large frying pan, add the garlic and cook for a minute or two, without browning. Add the sliced ceps and cook over gentle heat for about 5 minutes. Stir in the cream, then the basil leaves, roughly torn, and the walnuts. Season with salt and plenty of black pepper. Drain the spaghetti and pour over the mushroom sauce. Serve immediately.

SERVES 4

14 oz/400 g spaghetti
2 oz/50 g unsalted butter
1 large or 2 small cloves
garlic, finely chopped
8 oz/225 g ceps, sliced
10 fl oz/300 ml single cream
handful basil leaves
2 oz/50 g walnuts, roughly
chopped
salt and freshly ground
black pepper

Common yellow brittle gills

Pan-fried chicken with mushrooms and Marsala

SERVES 4

4 boneless chicken breasts
2 tbs olive oil
1 oz/25 g unsalted butter
2 shallots, finely chopped
8 oz/225 g mushrooms,
chopped small
1 tbs flour
5 fl oz/150 ml beef stock
1 tsp sage, chopped
5 fl oz/150 ml Marsala
5 fl oz/150 ml single cream
salt and freshly ground
black pepper

Both Madeira and Marsala go very well with mushrooms, and with chicken, although this rich, deeply flavoured sauce could also accompany kidneys, veal, steak or gammon.

Heat the oil and butter in a frying pan, and brown the chicken quickly over a high heat. Remove the chicken and keep warm, then add the shallots and mushrooms to the pan and cook gently for about 5 minutes. Stir in the flour, then pour on stock and add the sage. Bring to the boil, stirring, and allow to bubble for 5 minutes before adding the Marsala and cooking for a few minutes more. Season with salt and pepper, and return the chicken to the pan. Turn the heat down to moderate, and cook for about 20 minutes until the chicken is done. Carefully stir in the cream, heat through, and serve.

251

Safety code

There is no single test of the edibility of a mushroom – many of the 'popular' tests are based upon superstition alone. Each mushroom must be accurately identified.

• First learn to recognize the poisonous species, and be absolutely sure of your identification.

• Learn from an expert in the field during the mushroom season. A field-guide can only contain a limited number of species and cannot show the full variation, which may depend upon rain, heat, sunlight, shade, or unusual growing situations.

• To ensure correct identification, always carefully collect the whole fruitbody, including the base of the stem.

• Make a note of the habitat, soil and any tree with which the mushroom seems to be associated.

• Remember that different species may grow in close proximity and careless collecting could result in a mixture of species.

• Only collect young, fresh fruitbodies for eating. Always ignore old, decaying and mouldy specimens.

• Never collect near roads or industrial areas, as mushrooms can readily absorb heavy metals, such as lead.

• Carry your collections home in a well-aerated container, such as a rattan basket. Avoid placing specimens in polythene bags or enclosed containers. Keep the species separate. Always wash your hands after handling fungi.

• Always carefully clean the specimens and remove any soil particles. Slice the mushrooms to check for insect damage and maggots.

• Keep mushrooms in a cool, dry position, ideally in a refrigerator. They deteriorate rapidly and should be eaten within 24 hours.

• Do not eat raw mushrooms. Never eat a known edible species if it has been mixed with poisonous species in your collecting basket. If trying a wild mushroom for the first time then
(a) only take a small sample, (b) do not mix with other species, and (c) retain one fruitbody in case poisoning results and identification needs to be confirmed.

• Seek medical help immediately when poisoning is suspected.

LEGAL ASPECTS OF MUSHROOM PICKING IN BRITAIN

1 Trespass is a civil offence in England and Wales, but prosecution can really only succeed if real damage is caused. It is a more serious offence in Scotland.

2 Persistent trespassing, however, can lead to the landowner taking out an injunction ordering you to stop. Ignoring the order could lead to a fine or imprisonment (Contempt of Court Act, 1981).

3 'A person who picks mushrooms growing wild on any land..., does not steal what he picks, unless he does it for reward or for sale or for other commercial purpose... For the purpose of this section "mushroom" includes any fungus'. (Theft Act, 1968).

4 The intentional uprooting of any plant without authorization is prohibited (*The Wildlife and Countryside Act, 1981*). 'Uprooting' with regard to fungi could clearly be contentious.

5 Many nature sites have their own local bylaws, which may prohibit the collection of fungi (or forest produce).

6 Avoid offering poisonous mushrooms for consumption to another individual. Unlawful and malicious administration by any person of any destructive or noxious thing to endanger life, inflict grievous bodily harm, injure, aggrieve or annoy any person is prohibited (*Offences against the Person Act, 1961*).

7 The hunting for poisonous mushrooms with such intent, even if unsuccessful, is an offence (*Criminal Attempts Act, 1981*).

8 If you take a friend with you on such an expedition (see 7), both of you are guilty of conspiracy to administer (*Criminal Law Act, 1977*).

9 Voluntarily eating a poisonous mushroom infringes *The Suicide Act, 1961*.

10 The possession of controlled drugs without permission is unlawful (Section 5 (1) of the *Misuse of Drugs Act, 1971*). Drugs such as psilocin ('magic mushrooms'), lysergamide, lysergide (*Claviceps purpurea sclerotia*), and bufotenine (*Amanita pantherina*) are included in Schedule 2 of the Act, which is a list placing the drugs into three classes. The drugs found in mushrooms fall into Class A, the most severe offences. The Act further restricts all stereo-isomorphic forms, esters, ethers and salts of these substances. Further, possession of any 'preparation or other product containing a substance in the List' is also liable to prosecution. The term 'preparation', however, remains ambiguous.

Index of common and Latin names

Index of common and Latin names